MATAMOROS AND THE TEXAS REVOLUTION

By Craig H. Roell

TEXAS STATE
HISTORICAL ASSOCIATION
DENTON

Cover: The city of Matamoros, Tamaulipas, from a sketch by Lucius Avery, the U.S. commercial agent in Matamoros. Note the original Moroccan-style towers of the Cathedral of Our Lady of the Refuge dominating the skyline. *Frank Leslie's Illustrated Newspaper* (1863). From author's collection.

Library of Congress Cataloging-Publication Data

Roell, Craig H.
  Matamoros and the Texas Revolution / by Craig H. Roell.
  (Number twenty-three in the Fred Rider Cotten popular history series)
  Includes bibliographical references.
  ISBN 978-0-87611-260-1
1. Matamoros Expedition (1835–1836) 2. Matamoros (Tamaulipas, Mexico)—History—19th century. 3. Texas—History—Revolution, 1835–1836. I. Title. II. Series: Fred Rider Cotten popular history series ; no. 23.
  F390.R685 2013

CONTENTS

1. Introducing Matamoros: Pearl of Great Price   1

2. Envisioning Matamoros: Refuge among the Estuaries   18

3. Puerta Matamoros: Gateway to Texas, the Gulf ...and the World   27

4. Patriótica Matamoros: Revolution in Texas   38

5. Planning a Brilliant Folly: The Texan Expedition   47

6. Judas, Scoundrels, Wolves, and Rascally Acquirements   58

7. Triumphant Matamoros: The Mexican Expedition   68

8. Epilogue: Heróica Matamoros   87

Notes   94

Acknowledgments   111

About the Author   113

Index   114

To Melinda, Emily, and Nicole
(Psalms 37:3−5)

1.

INTRODUCING MATAMOROS: PEARL OF GREAT PRICE

Lo que nada cuesta, nada vale (Whatever costs nothing is worth nothing).
—Spanish proverb

"MATAMOROS LIES IN A PLAIN exposed to all winds; those most frequently prevailing are the North and South, which may be called prevalent."[1] These words of Mexican physician Dr. Antonio Lafon, in an otherwise mundane nineteenth-century medical report concerning yellow fever in Matamoros, Tamaulipas, provide a tempting metaphor for the magnetism of this bustling city on the lower Rio Grande, which historically has drawn to itself the "prevailing winds" from north and south, figuratively speaking. As such, the city offers an exceptional view for the Texas Revolution, an understanding that is essentially unappreciated north of the river. Cosmopolitan and international, Matamoros was economically strategic as a commercial center and port by the late 1820s, not just to the local and upriver ranching settlements and towns—the Villas del Norte—but to the larger northeastern regions of Tamaulipas, Nuevo León, Coahuila, Chihuahua, and even beyond to Mexico's national economy, thanks to ever-increasing trade revenue for goods brought from Europe and the United States, particularly New Orleans. The merchants of Matamoros brought the northern region of Mexico into permanent contact with the market economy of the United States, often with dramatic and unintended consequences still relevant today.

Tossed about in the feverish political disputes blowing northward from Mexico City and blowing southward from Texas and the United States, Matamoros was certainly "exposed to all winds." Vital to the dwellers of Mexico's northeastern frontier communities upriver—the *norteños*[2]—and to the many ranchos on the Rio Grande's banks, the port city was also important to Texas settlements served by the famous Matamoros-La Bahía Road. San Patricio, Refugio, La Bahía (Goliad) and Victoria were populated by Tejano and Irish colonists and increasingly by norteamericanos—Anglo Americans pouring into Texas from the United States—who rou-

I

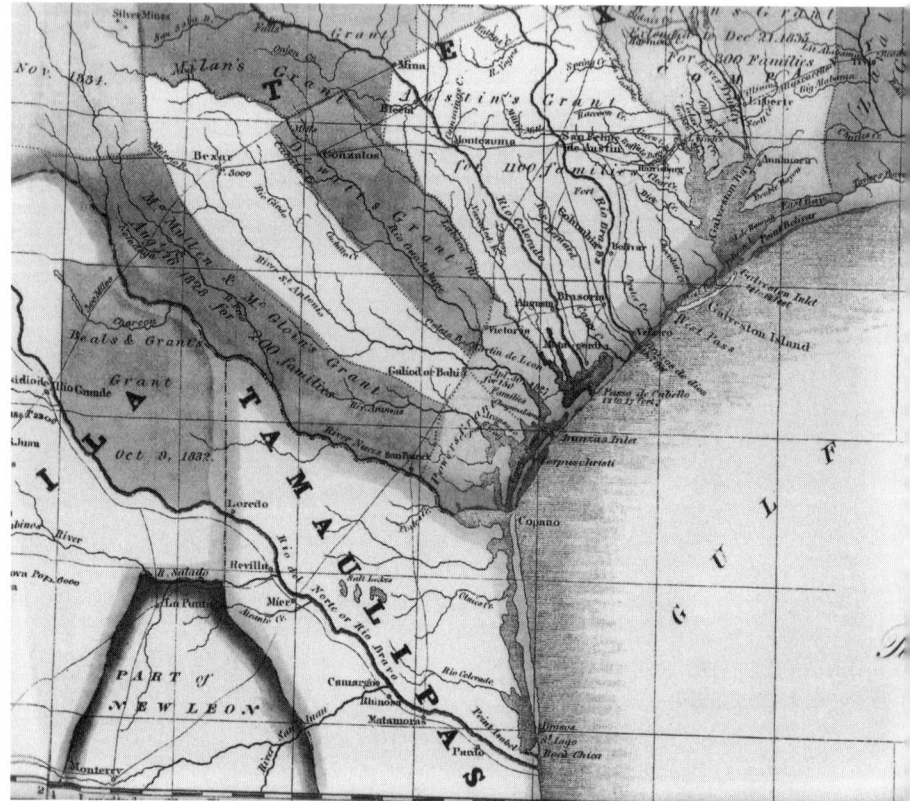

Map detail from *Texas, By David H. Burr*, cartographer (J. H. Colton & Co., New York, 1835). Note the road connecting Matamoros to the other Villas del Norte (Reynosa, Camargo, Mier, Laredo, Guerrero) along the Rio Bravo in Tamaulipas, the proximity of Point Isabel to Matamoros, the empresario grants in Texas north of the Nueces River, and the towns of San Patricio, Goliad (La Bahía), and Victoria on the Matamoros-La Bahía Road. *Courtesy Maps of the Past, Inc.* From author's collection.

tinely misspelled the city's heroic name, most commonly as "Matamoras" (as in Doctor Lafon's report, published in New Orleans).[3] The prevailing "winds" converged especially violently at Matamoros during the first half of the nineteenth century in several guises. Destructive hurricanes and cyclones in 1835 and 1837 pounded the Matamoros area, punctuating the political upheavals and civil war between Mexican centralists and federalists, the recurring attacks from Comanche Indians, and—the focus of this book—the troubles in Texas that ultimately resulted in the 1835–36 revolution in which Matamoros played a pivotal but unappreciated role.

Following the Mexican defeat at San Jacinto and the creation of an independent republic by Texan rebels, Matamoros served as a launching point for Mexico's unsuccessful attempts to reclaim Texas. The ravages of another severe hurricane in 1844 were but a prelude to a terribly costly and controversial war with the United States. The first battles of that conflict, at Palo Alto and Resaca de la Palma in 1846, occurred near Matamoros. Both ended in disastrous defeat for the Mexican army, resulting in the humiliating occupation of the city by the contemptible "*invasión Yanqui.*" But by the time Doctor Lafon wrote his medical report in 1853, Matamoros had redeemed the nation's reputation and elevated its own when it "heroically defended" against more revolutionaries—this time those attempting to establish an independent federalist Republic of the Sierra Madre (or Rio Grande), which the Mexican government feared was yet another episode in the decades-long menace of expansionist Manifest Destiny from the United States. The city's actions resulted in the state and federal congresses conferring the titles of "Unconquered" (*Invicta*), "Loyal" (*Leal*), and "Heroic" (*Heróica*), the latter signified by the letter "H" in city's formal name, "H. Matamoros."

The city's connection to the Texas Revolution—notably the Matamoros expedition of 1835–36—is not generally well known; moreover, the story is customarily enveloped in a traditional interpretation that this book seeks to redress. In the traditional story, insurgents in Texas resisting Mexican dictatorial president Santa Anna conspired to invade Matamoros in hopes of confiscating the port's considerable revenues for the Texas provisional government, fund their revolution, and occupy the city. By securing this lucrative jewel, the rebels hoped to negotiate a peace advantageous to Texas. The plan, initially launched with the support of Stephen F. Austin, Sam Houston, and the Texas provisional government, involved allying with Mexican federalist forces also distraught over Santa Anna's centralist policies in order to take the rebellion deeper into the Mexican interior and out of Texas altogether. The expedition is usually credited to (or blamed on) Dr. James Grant and Francis W. Johnson, who organized the trek in San Antonio after defeating Gen. Martín Perfecto de Cos's centralist force in the siege of Béxar. Such an action, they contended, would motivate the Texan forces, which consisted mainly of armed volunteers from the United States, and keep them engaged—especially with the potential of spoils. Nevertheless, the expedition quickly led to controversy and division. Historically lost amid the great dramas of the Alamo, Goliad, and San Jacinto, the Matamoros expedition's complexity and controversy have made it difficult to summarize—"there has always been in the minds of many, a confusion of ideas about what has been known as the Johnson and Grant expedition," wrote John Henry Brown in his 1892 classic *History of Texas*.[4] As the story goes, Johnson and Grant "stripped" the Alamo of men, equipment, and provisions for their ill-conceived expedition, then proceeded to Goliad, Refugio, and San Patricio en route to Matamoros. Houston became convinced that the expedition was a recipe for disaster. Failing in his attempt take command of the expedition, he at least convinced many of Johnson and Grant's men to remain at Refugio. Meanwhile, James W. Fannin recruited his own force (including a large contingent of volunteers from his home state of Georgia), which would also converge at Refugio. Houston's prediction proved true: the remnant of Johnson and Grant's expedition met defeat at the hands of the "invading" centralist Mexican army commanded by Gen. José de Urrea—Johnson at San Patricio and Grant at Agua Dulce Creek—in part due to their betrayal by "deceitful" Mexican federalists and Tejanos. Upon learning of Johnson and Grant's fate, Fannin abandoned Refugio to make a stand at Goliad in its old presidio (La Bahía), which he renamed Fort Defiance. After an aborted attempt to relieve William B. Travis at the Alamo, Fannin's own army met defeat against General Urrea in the battle of Coleto (Encinal del Perdido) while engaged in an ill-prepared retreat to Victoria that Houston had ordered. Fannin and his captured men were then executed under Santa Anna's orders and the "treachery" of Urrea in the infamous Goliad Massacre. Traditionally, the Matamoros expedition is dismissed as folly, a doomed venture from the outset—a view primarily informed by Houston's own interpretation.

Readers already familiar with the Matamoros expedition may presume this story is old news. Yet, as this book shows, the story is more complex in reality, comprising several different and even conflicting expeditions rather than simply one. Taken together, the Texan attempt to occupy the river city must be regarded as one of the most disastrous components of the Texas Revolution. It paralyzed the Texas provisional government. It left Texas forces divided of purpose. It revealed the disadvantages of asserting independence for Texas instead of remaining loyal to the Mexican federalist Constitution of 1824. It exposed the lack of realism in the thinking of Texans, who on the one hand discounted reports warning of Santa Anna's approaching army, while on the other they relied on rumors of great numbers of volunteers arriving from the United States and massive support by federalists in the Mexican interior. Thus, the Matamoros expedition proved foremost in the tragic events leading to the defeat of Texas forces at the battles of the Alamo, San Patricio, Agua Dulce Creek, Refugio, and Coleto—disasters that led to the Goliad Massacre.[5]

By contrast, this book approaches these issues from a Mexican viewpoint and explains the crucial geographic and economic context that made control of Matamoros truly advantageous and desirable. Moreover, the traditional Texas view neither recognizes nor appreciates the centrality of Matamoros in Mexican strategy or that the Mexican government and army had their own Matamoros campaign, which contrasted sharply in its success compared to the Texan failure. Such a focus on Matamoros reveals a double paradox. This successful Mexican Matamoros campaign, which resulted in a profound Texan defeat, required temporary cooperation between otherwise belligerent Mexican federalists and centralists against an even greater foe—Anglo Texan rebellion aided by an influx of volunteers from the United States. However, this victory occurred even as the predominantly federalist matamorenses committed acts of revolt against their own government's army. How matamorenses courageously sought to remain loyal Mexicans standing against foreign invaders while also being politically and economically devoted to their locality and region as federalists in the face of Santa Anna's centralist policies is a poignant story unappreciated in traditional interpretations.

For most readers, Matamoros's role in the Texas Revolution will likely be novel. Traditional Texas history books, which informed generations of school-age readers from the late nineteenth century until at least the 1960s, typically oversimplified the story of the Texan Matamoros expedition, reflected Sam Houston's interpretation, or simply omitted the connection altogether.[6] Matamoros just does not resonate in the familiar mythos of the Texas Revolution as do San Antonio, Goliad, or San Jacinto—it had no legendary "line in the sand," no dreadful "fight to the death," no infamous "massacre," no battle cry to "remember." Neither does it yowl controversy like "How did Davy die?" nor "To whom was this sacrifice useful?" It may seem marginal, distant, even inconsequential. After all, isn't Matamoros in Mexico? (Well remember, so was Texas!) So it might be surprising that the central theme of this book is that Matamoros was not simply important, but pivotal, being an essential link in the divisive, muddled, audacious, reckless, infuriating, controversial, and yes, heroic story of the Texas Revolution. In addition, this book shows how Matamoros was also central to Mexico's own strategies to preserve Texas, to suppress the rebellion, to retake Texas after San Jacinto, and then to defend the homeland in the war with the United States following the annexation of Texas.

Histories of the Texas Revolution abound. But as historian Jack Jackson once remarked, "The problem—as I learned after doing my book on the Alamo—is that many people prefer the myth to the truth."[7] The traditional and still most widely familiar interpretations of the Texas Revolution tend to reflect (if not romanticize) an Anglo Texan point of view, focusing on the deteriorating relationship between Anglo and Mexican authorities, the differences (even incompatibilities) between American and Mexican culture and ethnicity, and the "collective memory" about the heroes and martyrs of Anglo nation-building.[8] Remembering the Alamo and Goliad and celebrating San Jacinto are key components of this tradition. But as historian Andrés Reséndez observed, "This is only the last leg of a much longer saga of successive revolutions" that erupted in the northern Mexican states, not just in Texas.[9]

Another school of thought popular among American, Mexican, and European historians puts the Texas Revolution in the larger context of Manifest Destiny as the United States expanded its dominion across the continent. Robert May, for example, called the Texas Revolution "the most successful filibuster in American history." Stuart Reid even more provocatively proposed that while the revolution was certainly "an off-shoot to a much wider Mexican civil war," it ultimately was part of a twenty-year-long "secret war" between London and Washington "to secure mastery of the North American continent."[10] Reid argued that a Matamoros expedition may have been part of the British government's "grand project" against American imperialism and asserted that the expedition and its supposedly disreputable leader, Dr. James Grant, are not so easily dismissed as historians—most taking their cue from Sam Houston's censuring judgment of the affair—have summarily done.

Other recent approaches, such as Reséndez's, build upon David J. Weber's outstanding contributions and venture a balanced Mexican point of view.[11] These historians focus, for one example, on how independence movements in Texas and elsewhere on the northern frontier were fueled by Mexico's internal political strife and economic challenges as well as the pull of the United States' market economy. For another example, these scholars provide new avenues for exploring the complexities of colonial Texas, such as intermarriage between Anglos and Mexicans or how Mexican Texans believed they could be both proud mexicanos and loyal Tejanos. Still another approach explores the ambiguities of constructing a national identity that was not simply Mexican or Anglo American, as if either were somehow monolithic. Moreover, this more balanced approach has vividly demonstrated how preconceived notions, racism, bowdlerizing and mistranslation of sources, and misplaced idealism have contributed to mythmaking about the Texas Revolution, particularly the Alamo story.[12] Not surprisingly, these recent writers have garnered deserved praise but also passionate criticism (notably on Amazon.com) for "destroying Texas history." Writing from Matamoros in 1836, the controversial Mexican "eye-witness to the Texas Revolution," Lt. Col. José Enrique de la Peña, well understood such risks. "I am well aware how difficult it is to write for the public and to fulfill the mission of a historian."[13] It is my hope that this focus on Matamoros in the Texas Revolution will provide an innovative yet balanced perspective on what may seem like an old tale.

Matamoros was the flash point for six major movements by 1835: (1) Mexican centralists hoping to defend Mexico's territorial sovereignty; (2) federalists in Mexico (including Texas) hoping to establish Texas as a new federalist Mexican state, or more radically, even as part of an independent federalist republic of the Rio Grande; (3) Tejano, Irish, and Anglo Texans vying with each other and with incoming volunteers and filibusters from the United States over the identity and destiny of Texas; (4) U.S. expansionist strategies; (5) Mexican and perhaps British designs to thwart U.S. encroachment; (6) and not least, the changing identities and conflicting actions of matamorenses themselves. To return to the opening metaphor, the converging winds of the Texas Revolution swept Matamoros from both north and south precisely because of the city's centrality.

Matamoros could not have occupied this principal position, however, by being merely a strategic city swept up in Texas's revolutionary turmoil. Its reputation, closely allied to its crucial location near the mouth of the legendary Río Bravo (as the Spaniards called the lower Rio Grande), was built over a century of Spanish and then Mexican developments, particularly in trade, ranching, and the church.[14] Award-winning writer Arturo Zárate-Ruiz does not exaggerate in describing Matamoros as "the historic and cultural center of the Rio Grande Valley or 'Bajo Bravo.'" It is why today the city of Matamoros calls itself *La Gran Puerta de México* (The Great Gateway of Mexico). In the city's Parque Cultural Olímpico (Olympic Cultural Park) in 2007, workers constructed a gigantic, towering metal sculpture, vividly painted red, in the shape of an abstract elongated letter *M* designed to represent the city and the nation as well as beams of celestial light. Affixed in the letter's apex is an intricate, multidimensional "starry" cube, representing "intrinsic strength" and "dynamism" of the city. World-renowned artist Sebastián (Enrique González Carbajal) designed the sculpture to celebrate the city's self-proclaimed historic place—its "ancient truth" (*realidad ancestral*), as the distinguished Mexican historian Octavio Herrera Pérez puts it—as the dual "opening toward Mexico and the world." The monumental sculpture dominates the skyline and is located on "the original site of Matamoros," which sits, not by chance, in "a privileged area because of its vicinity with two international bridges" crossing the legendary river.[15]

The sculpture brims with the lofty expectations that Matamoros has been able to command in Mexican history. Long before it was renamed in 1826 to honor Mariano Matamoros (1770–1814), the Mexican priest

D. MARIANO MATAMOROS.

*Cura interino del Pueblo de Jantetelco en 1810; abnegado y fiel amigo del cau-
dillo Morelos, dedicó su valor y su inteligencia á defender la independencia
de su patria. Murió fusilado en Valladolid el 3 de Febrero de 1814.*

Lit. de la V. de Murguía é hijos.

Father Mariano Matamoros (1770–1814), warrior-priest and martyred hero of Mexico's War of Independence, and the man for whom Matamoros was renamed. Manuel Rivera Cambas, *Los gobernantes de México* (1873), appendix. From author's Collection.

and hero in Mexico's War of Independence from Spain, the area of Matamoros was an important Indian and later Spanish camping site among the innumerable sabal palm trees lining the river. When the site was named—perhaps as early as 1686, but certainly by 1706—its Spanish moniker first signified the many "beautiful estuaries" (*esteros hermosos*) dotting the area, resulting from the wild river's periodic flooding. Stalwart pioneer families, lured by the river and estuaries, established large ranchos along both sides the Río Bravo, literally *con un pie en cada lado*, with a foot on each side of river. We should remember that at this time the lower Rio Grande was a much wilder river and did not divide countries, but was rather "merely an obstacle for ranchers with lands and cattle on both sides of its banks."[16] In 1774, these ranching families established a headquarters settlement, located approximately in present-day downtown Matamoros at Fifth and Matamoros Streets, naming it San Juan de los Esteros Hermosos to honor Saint John in addition to the estuaries. The settlement was later rechristened as Refugio (Refuge) by ever-hopeful Catholic Franciscan missionaries, who established a church—really a rather modest chapel—in 1793.[17]

In time, the growing village supported a flourishing ranching culture that thrived on the wild mustang horses and longhorn cattle of what is now the South Texas grassland prairies. Farming in the rich river bottoms of the Río Bravo supplied corn and eventually cotton and sugarcane. The village's then unimposing chapel and modest alcalde's residence of adobe brick with palm roof faced a main plaza called the Plaza de Armas. The name of the plaza referred to its military purpose: to store weapons and serve as a defense against marauding bandits and Indians, particularly Comanches. This layout was a model in use in Spanish settlements throughout the Americas. Construction of the plaza's earthen fortifications, chains, and iron gates started about 1800. The Río Bravo's great flood of 1814 caused the plaza and town center, including the chapel and municipal building, to be moved 220 yards (200 meters) south to their present location, bounded by four streets eventually named Calle Real (now Sixth Street), Calle Comercio (now González), Calle de Terán (now Fifth) and Calle Morelos (still so named). By 1831, the east side of the plaza was graced by the completion of the architecturally magnificent Catedral de Nuestra Señora del Refugio (Cathedral of Our Lady of Refuge) as well as a more stately two-story municipal government building (*la presidencia municipal*) on the west side. Today, the plaza remains the city's center as a beautiful park and popular gathering place called Plaza Hidalgo. The plaza is still bordered by the municipal building, a variety of businesses, and the cathedral—the current pointed steeples, which are constructed in the French Creole style popular in New Orleans, differ considerably from the original rounded Moroccan-style towers that dominated the city's skyline during the troubles with Texas in the 1830s and 1840s.

Prospering international trade resulted in the establishment of a customs house (*aduana*) in 1823 to collect valuable revenues. The building was ultimately located on the main plaza and beside the church. The Mexican government keenly saw Matamoros's commerce and tariff revenue as vital in salvaging the national economy, which was devastated by the recent War of Independence from Spain. Matamoros quickly became the third most important Mexican port on the Gulf of Mexico after Veracruz and Tampico. The city was crucial to the entire northeastern region, functioning as a critical commercial connection to New Orleans and Europe. Indeed, by the time of the insurrection in Texas, Matamoros funneled two-thirds of the goods imported to the region north of Guadalajara and Querétero.

Matamoros's importance lay not only in its economic or military assets, but also its ability to stir the imagination. The promise of substantial trade revenues through the Matamoros customs house generated passionate schemes throughout the northern provinces, first among Mexican federalists primarily in Tamaulipas, Nuevo León, and Coahuila, then in revolutionary Texas, where several plots were concocted for alliance with or the capture of the river city. Indeed, in the aftermath of Mexican independence from Spain (1821), such growth had stirred the government to grant the village of Refugio the new status of "town" (*villa*) in 1825. The Tamaulipas government renamed the town in 1826 to honor the Mexican insurgent priest and revolutionary soldier, Father Mariano Matamoros, the martyred lieutenant general who had been posthumously awarded the title of *Benemérito de la Patria* (national hero). The town's new name also had deeper meanings, summoning religious and cultural references to the Spanish warrior-saint Santiago Matamoros. Only a few years later, the government granted Villa de Matamoros the higher rank of "city" (*ciudad*), recognizing that it had indeed become a strategic center of trade, commerce, ranching, religion, politics, and international relations.

Names carry intrinsic meanings, some obvious and some veiled. Certainly, the renaming and elevation of Congregación de Refugio to Villa de Matamoros in 1826 did indeed honor the warrior-priest and martyred hero of Mexican independence, Mariano Matamoros. *Fronterizos* (people of the frontier) similarly rechristened other municipalities in Tamaulipas and Nuevo León.[18] But lurking in the historical background of the Matamoros name is a more complicated allusion to Santiago (Saint James the Greater), patron saint of the Spanish *Reconquista*. According to tradition, Santiago's miraculous military intervention, charging on a white horse while slaying the enemy with his deadly sword, gave Ramiro of Castile's forces victory over the Muslims at the Battle of Clavijo circa 844 AD. With Santiago's continued intervention, Spaniards successfully drove the Muslim invaders (also called "Moors") from the Iberian Peninsula. Because of this help, Spaniards gave the saint the honorific title of "Mata Moros"—"Killer of Moors." In a later century, Cervantes had Don Quixote proclaim, "San-

Saint James the Great as Santiago Matamoros (Saint James the Moor Slayer), legendary conqueror of the enemies of Spain and later Mexico and the ultimate inspiration in the renaming of Matamoros. Illustration after Juan Carreño de Miranda's painting of 1660. Anna Jameson, *Sacred and Legendary Art* (1898), 237. From author's collection.

tiago Mata Moros [St. James the Moor Slayer], one of the most valiant saints and knights which earth ever produced, or heaven now contains. . . . You must know, that God has given this great knight with a red cross, as a patron and protector to Spain."[19]

By the sixteenth century, the patron warrior-saint was further transformed and called upon against numerous enemies of Catholic Spain, especially in conquering the Americas and the malignity of its indigenous gods. Numerous geographic sites, towns, and settlements were named Santiago (more than eighty settlements in Mexico alone), and festivals and pageants honoring Santiago Matamoros were celebrated throughout Latin America, particularly on the dangerous frontier. As historians Milo Kearney and Manuel Medrano have shown, "The culture of the Mexican-American Borderlands," including historic Anglo-Hispanic tensions, misunderstandings, and hostilities, "cannot be fully understood without knowledge of its medieval underpinnings in both Castile and in England," when the hostile stereotypes that Anglos and Hispanics held toward each other in the nineteenth century actually originated. Medieval culture influenced language, law, politics, economics and social class, literature, art, music, architecture, and especially religion. Indeed, they assert,

RANCHEROS.

Rancheros, the pioneers of Matamoros, the Bajo Bravo, and South Texas, renowned in their ranching skills, and honorable civilian soldiers under Gen. Urrea during the Texas Revolution. Illustration probably after *Rancheros 1834*, hand-colored lithograph by Carl Nebel, in *Voyage pittoresque et archéologique dans la partie la plus intéressante du Mexique* (1836), reproduced in Brantz Mayer, *Mexico; Aztec, Spanish and Republican, Vol. II* (1853), following p. 22. From author's collection.

"the religious flavor of Borderlands society is its strongest tie to the Middle Ages."[20]

Accordingly, Saint James, in the guise of Santiago Matamoros, became the champion for the common people and especially for the soldiers in the Spanish colonial era. His iconography, which featured him astride his horse raising his sword amid the fray, became ubiquitous in Mexico's northeastern region, most conspicuously in the Bajo Bravo. The venerable founder of the norteño settlements, José de Escandón, was a "Vowed Knight of the Order of Santiago," or more properly, the Military Order of St. James of the Sword, as was Juan Armando de Palacio of the Royal Commission to the Colonies of Nuevo Santander, who allotted the land grants to the colonists and laid out Matamoros's sister towns upriver: Camargo, Reynosa, Mier, and Laredo. Not surprisingly in this isolated frontier society, which valued political autonomy and by necessity organized alliances to defend against enemy Indians and outsiders, the esteemed rancheros emerged as the vital citizen militia to become heroic defenders in the spirit of Saint James. Churches throughout the lower Rio Grande Valley encouraged this association.

As matamorenses faced war with the Comanches, insurgents in Texas, and increasing threats from the United States, they did not lose sight of the warrior-saint in the official renaming of their community to honor of the warrior-priest. As much as the village had indeed once been a "refuge," it was now time for the city, growing ever more vital to the national economy and security, to take on the trappings of the warrior. In their very name, matamorenses did not just honor the warrior-priest, projecting patriotism and courage, but subtly invoked the power of the warrior-saint against invaders. When Thomas Bangs Thorpe published his memoir, *Our Army on the Rio Grande*, in 1846, he would write that the renaming of Refugio to Matamoros "would have been considered most honorable indeed, by the Spaniards who conquered the Alhambra, as the name of the city signified that its inhabitants had distinguished themselves in the wars with the Moors."[21]

About the time of its name change, the great military importance of Matamoros became evident. The government sought to protect precious trade revenue against increasing threats not only from Indians, bandits, and pirates but also against an attempted reinvasion of Mexico by Spain in July 1829. These challenges were accompanied by rising political unrest from interior Mexico and from Texas. Early in 1830, President Anastasio Bustamante named Gen. José Manuel de Mier y Terán commandant general of the Eastern Interior Provinces to supervise political and military affairs in Texas, Coahuila, Nuevo León, and Tamaulipas. Significantly, the general headquartered in Matamoros, where he also installed the new office of collector of customs and remained ever wary of U.S. expansionist designs on Texas. General Mier y Terán ordered construction of more formal fortifications to defend the city increasingly viewed as the Bajo Bravo's pearl of great price. Complementing the protection naturally afforded by the river and its characteristic resacas and wetland estuaries, the fortification project began in 1832 under Gen. Mariano Paredes y Arrillaga and Matamoros alcalde Juan Nepomuceno Molano with the construction of a strong wall next to the river near the Paso de la Anacuita ferry crossing. In 1835, Fort Guerrero was built specifically to face a threatened invasion from Texas.[22] Matamoros eventually featured a series of fortifications encompassing the city reminiscent of other Latin American seaports—Veracruz, Havana, and Cartagena—based on the idea of the European walled city. Today, little remains of the fortifications except for the restored Casamata, which houses the City Archives and Museum. Unusual in Mexico, this imposing ring undoubtedly added a romantic old world dimension to the city's mystique.[23]

Even though Matamoros was not opened as a legal port by Mexican law until 1826, foreign merchants—English, American, French, Irish, Italian, German—had already established businesses there to promote and take advantage of the promising commercial atmosphere, which had been encouraged by the Spanish government in 1820 in an effort to collect revenue from the already lucrative smuggling trade. The city's rising prominence can be seen in the words and action of the noted French naturalist Jean Louis Berlandier, who made several botanical collecting trips into Mexico and Texas between 1826 and 1834. Berlandier described Matamoros before Mexico's independence from Spain (1821) as "nothing but a large, little-known hamlet," whose inhabitants "lived off the produce of their herds and their wretched agriculture," with its port "not frequented even by vessels which carried on cabotage along the coasts of the Gulf." Yet, Berlandier himself was charmed by the city's promise, for in 1829 he became a resident of Matamoros, where he married and set up practice as a physician. Moreover, by 1831 he called his adopted hometown "one of the principal trading centers of Tamaulipas."[24] Although the present condition of the Rio Grande would seem to belie this appraisal, we must remember that in the early nineteenth century, as historian David Montejano reminds us, "the greatest expectations of the commercially minded settlers were pinned on that river," which promised to connect the Chihuahua-Santa Fe trade with the Gulf of Mexico and even to the world. Thus, the Rio Grande was easily compared to the Mississippi or the Hudson rivers, with Matamoros commanding the gateway. It is not without significance that the United States Consulate in Matamoros, first established in 1836, is the oldest continuously active post in the U.S. Foreign Service.[25]

Matamoros was indeed an economically important port, a trade and ranching center, a political hub, a fortified city and military garrison, site of an inspiring cathedral, a beloved home, and a place of refuge amid the "beautiful estuaries," but Matamoros was much more. Ultimately, Matamoros in 1835 must be seen as a motivation, a longing, and a hope. "Opulent" was the way veteran Texas revolutionary soldier Creed Taylor would remember the city; it was the vital port of entry "for a vast territory embracing a quarter part of Old Mexico and all of New Mexico." Matamoros was a "great maritime mart" for merchants coming from Santa Fe, Taos, Paso del Norte, Monclova, Monterrey, and Chihuahua, while home to "Spanish hidalgos and Mexican dons" who "reveled in oriental splendor." Completing this Edenic scene, Taylor recounted how "grass, game, wild cattle and horses abounded" in the flatland prairie stretching between Matamoros and the Texas settlements.[26] The city, with its legalized port and new name, became a passionate symbol of Mexican independence and the promise of a "new Mexico" under federalism, as well as the simultaneous end of commercial and social isolationism previously imposed by the government-sanctioned trade monopoly that Veracruz once enjoyed. Creed Taylor's alluring description was not uncommon. The area "is one of the most desirable spots on the face of the earth," echoed the author of *Mexico versus Texas, a Descriptive Novel*, in 1838. William Kennedy's *Texas*, perhaps the single best work published on Texas during the Republic period, predicted in 1841 that "the port of Matamoros . . . would thus in the course of no very considerable period become the New Orleans and the Rio Grande the Mississippi of this part of the world."[27]

At the time of Matamoros's ascent to prominence in the 1820s and 1830s, "Texas fever" was sweeping the Mexican province to the north as immigrants rushed from the United States and elsewhere in to acquire land. Historian Graham Davis rightly emphasized that the "central preoccupation with land" is "a consistent theme running through all the events of the Texas Revolution and among those who lived through it." Land was the most attractive and most marketed motivation that brought settlers—both legal and illegal—to Texas.[28] Colonists began arriving at Stephen F. Austin's colony on the Brazos River in December 1821, and the settlement of immigrants, mostly from the southern United States, thrived. Impressed by the success of Austin's colony, the Mexican government passed new colonization laws creating an empresario system as part of a defensive strategy to preserve Texas for Mexico against foreign powers and to help buffer the Río Bravo settlements against increasing Indian attacks.[29] Austin's masterful diplomacy and tireless effort to build trust among the Mexicans coincided with federalists gaining victory over their rivals and their creation of a government under the federal Constitution of 1824. In theory, the federalist colonization laws would quickly construct, through enormous opportunities for land ownership, a hardworking population of naturalized citizens loyal to Mexico. Mexican empresarial contracts legitimized this process, promising to develop the land, trade, and fortunes, and gave some sense of governmental control. The constitution also created two new states: Tamaulipas and Coahuila y Tejas, with the Nueces River forming the boundary between the two. By 1835, forty-one empresario contracts were issued, resulting in colonies—at least on paper—stretching from the Nueces River to the border of Louisiana Territory, and Matamoros was to have a key role in "nationalizing" Texas for Mexico.

Nevertheless, most immigrants from the United States continued to enter into Texas illegally as squatters, ignoring international law and boundaries, and bypassing the empresario system. By mid-1836, the Anglo American population numbered 35,000 (including slaves)—about tenfold the number of Spanish-speaking Tejanos. This was the great paradox of Mexico's "solution" to the Texas problem: Mexico gained frontier residents by offering cheap land and populating the state with settlers from the United States, but the settlers' language, customs, and laws, were foreign to that of Hispanic Mexico and they harbored a deep prejudice against a people, a religion, and a culture they believed to be inferior. Of course, proud Tejanos and other norteños, many tracing their family heritage directly back to Spain, would return that sentiment, with many quickly coming to doubt the government's wisdom of saving Texas by bringing in arrogant, deceitful, uncouth, even vulgar norteamericanos, who seemed willing to sell anything in the name of profit. But the reality was that the Mexican military was too small and the frontier too large to police effectively against illegal aliens from the United States. Settlers from the United States were also set apart by their reliance on slavery, an institution that the Mexican government took steps to limit or abolish throughout the 1820s and 1830s. These steps, in turn, created resentment and fear among the colonists. This situation exacerbated the schism between the federalists, who favored a liberal colonization of Texas, and the centralists, ever wary of encroachment by the United States, who did not. This factional division, in historian Arturo Zárate-Ruiz's assessment "weakened [Mexicans] as a people, and made us easy prey to the greed of empires."[30]

Naturally, the government preferred and therefore encouraged Mexican settlers from the interior to move to Texas, but Mexicans remained reluctant to move to the northern frontier because of the region's remoteness and its Indian menace. The great exception was Martín De León's flourishing colony at Victoria on the Guadalupe River. With the advantage of Mexican citizenship, De León and his considerable extended family were a ranching enterprise that dominated the lower Guadalupe, and Lavaca river valleys as well as the government at La Bahía (Goliad), and they maintained direct connections with Matamoros. As wealthy and loyal Spanish Mexicans supporting federalism, De León's sons and sons-in-law would play significant roles in the Texas Revolution in support of the Constitution of 1824. Among them were Plácido Benavides, who would accompany Dr. James Grant on the ill-fated Matamoros expedition and send the warning, tragically unheeded, to James W. Fannin that the Mexican army under Gen. José de Urrea was en route to Goliad.[31]

The Irish also immigrated to Texas, some settling in De León's colony, notably John ("Juan") J. Linn. But most went to the predominantly Irish colonies below the Guadalupe at Refugio and San Patricio, which were naturally drawn into the orbit of Matamoros. The Irish colonies consisted of the Power and Hewetson colony at Refugio and the McMullen and

McGloin colony at San Patricio on the Nueces (the "last stop" on the La Bahía Road to Matamoros). The Mexican government viewed the Irish as offering much less risk as colonists than Anglo Americans in that they shared with Mexicans a common Roman Catholic faith. Having been targets of intense ethnic and religious prejudice in their native British Empire and in the United States, Irish colonists would also be less likely to hold attitudes of racial superiority over Mexicans or to favor coalition with Anglo Americans. Not surprisingly, Mexicans also settled in the Irish colonies and intermarriage was common. The Irish learned the skills and traditions of the ranching culture from their Mexican neighbors, how to survive and prosper on the raw frontier, and how to preserve and raise their families. Such cooperation was the hope of the Mexican government's strategy to preserve Texas for Mexico through colonization.

The empresarios who established Irish colonies in the crucial zone between the Guadalupe and Bravo Rivers became Mexican citizens and prosperous businessmen in Matamoros before undertaking their colonization enterprises. The residents of San Patricio and Matamoros enjoyed particularly close trade and social relationships, including an annual four-day fiesta, *El Lugar del Banquete,* hosted on the banks of Agua Dulce Creek just south of the Nueces; the site was named Banquete in commemoration. San Patricians tended to support the Mexican government against Texas independence, but ironically, some were captured and imprisoned in Matamoros by the Mexican army under General Urrea as a consequence of the Matamoros expeditions. One band of the expeditions led by Dr. James Grant would be defeated in the battle of Agua Dulce Creek, only about a mile from the festive site of Banquete.[32]

The story of Matamoros thus is altogether different than the one that nourished the memorable symbols of the Texas Revolution—the Alamo, Goliad, and San Jacinto. Rather, it was Matamoros—with its strategic history and geography, its proven economic, political, and military importance, its international connections and cosmopolitan society, and perhaps most of all, its potential—that supplied the driving force of extravagant expectations that undergirded the revolutionary expeditions. Of course there are other factors, but few today know the central role Matamoros played in the Texas Revolution and the Mexican response to it. To put it another way, while we remember the Alamo, Goliad, and San Jacinto, Matamoros has become forgotten in the traditional Texas story.

2.

ENVISIONING MATAMOROS: REFUGE AMONG THE ESTUARIES

TO SEE MATAMOROS AS THE GREAT GATEWAY to Mexico—the reason the city was so desirable to so many contestants in the Texas Revolution—requires an appreciation for its challenging geography, inviting appearance, and vital economics. It is hard to imagine how astonished early settlers must have been when they first encountered this rich and exotic land teeming with wildlife, a unique ecosystem of resacas, meandering streams, estuaries, mudflats, lomas, and clay dunes, its vegetation both severe and beautiful. Summers have historically been long and hot, droughts frequent, hurricanes threatening, and the otherwise mild winters disrupted by legendary biting "northers," whose rain and dramatically dropping temperatures were enemies faced by soldiers on both sides of the Texas Revolution.

Spaniards dubbed the lower course of the great river the Río Bravo, denoting "wild, bold, fierce, angry," terms prophetically suitable for the area's turbulent history. The sharp hairpin turns of the lower Bravo—which contributed both the river's historic wildness and its characteristic resacas—made it (in a phrase common among boatmen) "exceedingly tortuous" to navigate, even though the river measured about eighty yards in width and, varying according to the seasons, from seven to nine feet in depth for about one hundred miles from its mouth. While Matamoros was only about thirty-one miles (fifty kilometers) from the Gulf of Mexico, the anfractuous windings of the river nearly doubled that distance. Moreover, a sandbar at the entrance of the harbor, which only smaller vessels usually could negotiate, added to navigational hazards. Punta de Isabel (Point Isabel), established some twenty miles north overland, served Matamoros as a much-needed deep-water port, while Bagdad, established about half a mile from the Bravo's mouth, offered an unloading station for boats unable or unwilling to negotiate the winding river to unload at Matamoros itself. In both cases, cargo was unloaded and hauled to Matamoros by mule packs or oxcarts.

The dense and thorny brushland characterizing the lower Rio Grande

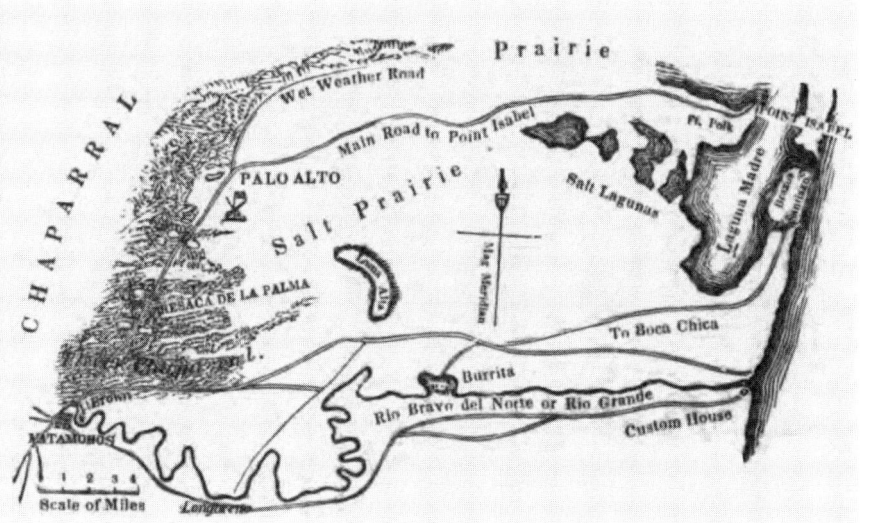

Map showing the area from Matamoros to Point Isabel (Punta de Isabel), which displays the "exceedingly tortuous" windings of the Río Bravo, the thick chaparral surrounding the roads to the deep-water port at Point Isabel and Boca Chica, and the customs hut at Bagdad near the river's mouth. Based on a map by Jean Louis Berlandier (1846). John Frost, *History of Mexico and Its Wars* (1882), 234. From author's collection.

Valley, bristling with plants like catclaw, horse killer, and crucifixion thorn, is aptly called thorn scrub; everything seems to have thorns, briars, stickers, or prickles. Kentuckian William A. McClintock put it vividly in his account of 1846–47: "40 miles from the river we entered the so called Rio Grand timber which is one continued and increasing chaparel of musquit Lignum vitae, long gigantic cactus (or prickly pear), with thousands of shrubs, and grasses, all bearing pricks, thorns, or burs. There is nothing of the vegitable world on the rio grand, but what is armed with weapons of defence, and offence."[1] In his colorful memoir, *The Twelve Months Volunteer* (1848), Tennessean George C. Furber echoed this assessment. In trekking from the Nueces River to Matamoros, Furber recounted the open prairie of marsh, short grasses, and even wild red pepper. Depending on the season, this coastal prairie could either be very muddy from rains or dangerously dry, with the traveler finding "tolerable water" only sporadically. The landscape changed dramatically upon entering chaparral. Unlike the openness of the prairie, Furber wrote, in the chaparral, "we were crowded up in narrow intervals, with thorns on every side; the close musquit being loaded with them, and the vast quantity of prickly pear covered with

Mexican muleteers (*arrieros*) transported goods from Matamoros to the Mexican interior, including the states of Tamaulipas, Nuevo León, San Luis Potosí, Zacatecas, Durango, and Chihuahua. Illustration after *Arrieros*, hand-colored lithograph by Carl Nebel, *Voyage pittoresque et archéologique dans la partie la plus intéressante du Mexique* (1836), reproduced in Brantz Mayer, *Mexico, As It Was and As It Is* (1847), following p. 18. From author's collection.

the same;—if we found a place of grass large enough to lay down, we bounced up again quicker than we threw ourselves down: for the grass was full of these burs, that were keener than needles." Moreover, "We also saw, rearing its head in the dense thicket, many trunks of the sword palmetto, or Spanish bayonet, from fifteen to twenty-five feet high;—this, like the prickly pear and the musquit tree, was to be in our constant view." Because of these armed plants, Furber acknowledged a great appreciation for Mexican ranchero attire. "It is customary, in the country, for Mexicans, when riding, to have a kind of false pantaloons [*chaparreras*], which buckle round the waist and go over each leg: these are made of goat skin, and have the hair on; they are sufficiently stout to withstand the penetration of the thorns; they are called *armor de pelo* (covering of hair), and when not used, hang to the saddle, in front of the leg." It was no wonder that men associated this unforgiving landscape with the host of hell, calling it "the d-v-l-sh chapparal."[2] German explorer-botanist Frederick Adolph Wislizenus observed the Matamoros area in 1846–47 as "endless chaparral" which "forms the constant companion." Frederick Law Olmsted, in his 1857 memoir, included a description of the landscape surrounding the very dusty road to Matamoros as "abandoned to hopeless chaparral."[3]

Nevertheless, the vegetation yielded a certain beauty and even utility. Cenizo ("purple sage"), like the ebony tree, could predict rain if blooming, according to folklore.[4] The ebony yielded seeds, which, like mesquite beans, provided a food source. The palmetto contributed thatch for the characteristic roofing of dwellings in the region. The maguey (agave) plant, which grew wild but also was cultivated, produced a sap that furnished distilled alcoholic beverages of pulque and mescal. The strong fibers in the plant's leaves were made into rope, sackcloth (*guangoche*), shoe thread, and sewing thread. The plant's upright shoot, when roasted and cut into pieces, was sweet like sugarcane and prized for chewing. The ubiquitous prickly pear cactus provided a celebrated food and medicine source for centuries. In his 1828 inspection of Texas, Gen. Manuel Mier y Terán noted that the prickly pear was "among the most abundant vegetation covering the land from Matamoros on the entire way we have traveled." He drew special attention to the *cochinilla*, a little red insect "found in abundance" on the cactus leaves; when dried, it "provides the best scarlet [dye] known." Another traveler, William B. Dewees, writing in 1827, commented on the difficulty and danger the cactus presented: "The road is ofttimes completely hedged in for miles by long rows of prickly pear, which are almost impassable. Beneath the huge leaves of the pear are vast quantities of snakes and poisonous reptiles, which have crawled under them to shelter themselves from the scorching rays of the sun." But Dewees also captured the beauty and especially the immensity of the

Carreta de bueyes (oxcart). The venerable oxen-pulled *carreta* brought trade goods to Matamoros from boats off-loading at the river port or at the coastal landings at Bagdad and Punta de Isabel. They dominated the cart road from Victoria and Goliad to San Patricio and Matamoros as well as the roads to the upriver Villas del Norte and to the Mexican interior. Note the planked rather than spoked wheels. Postcard from author's collection.

cactus, which "grows from one to fifteen feet in height, and frequently with a round body like a tree, eighteen inches in diameter, and the leaves measuring a foot in breadth. The flowers are red, yellow, and white; these are exceedingly beautiful and large. The fruit is sometimes blue, and sometimes red, and of a very pleasant flavor. . . . When these various cactuses are in full bloom with all their rich and varied hues, they render the prairies beautiful beyond the power of language to describe."[5]

This ancient geography sustained a rich wildlife. Migratory hunters, travelers, settlers, and soldiers found whitetail deer, antelope, javelina, and even bison, bobcats, ocelots, and jaguarundi. Coyote and smaller animals also flourished, including armadillo, jackrabbits, prairie dogs and squirrels, hog-nosed skunks, gophers, and a rich assortment of snakes, turtles, lizards, bats, rats and mice, insects, and birds, notably the noisy chachalaca (Mexican tree pheasant), named for its raucous, earsplitting "cha-cha-lac-a" group call. But most significant among the wildlife were the wild mustangs (*los mesteños*), having descended and multiplied from strays from bygone Spanish expeditions. These legendary horses became so plentiful that the plains between the Nueces and the Río Bravo were nicknamed "Llanos Mesteñas." One witness, John C. Duval, who survived the Goliad Massacre, observed in the 1840s "a drove of mustangs so large as it took us fully an hour to pass it, although they were traveling at a rapid rate in a direction nearly opposite to ours. As far as the eye could extend on a dead level prairie, nothing was visible except a dense mass of horses, and the trampling of their hoofs sounded like the roar of the surf on a rocky coast." Ulysses S. Grant, recalling his experience as a lieutenant under Gen. Zachary Taylor in 1846, similarly described an amazing scene a few days journey south of the Nueces: "As far as the eye could reach to our right, the herd extended. To the left, it extended equally. There was no estimating the number of animals in it."[6] It would be the crucial need for such horses that ostensibly drove elements of the ill-fated Matamoros expedition in the Texas Revolution.

Travelers coming upon Matamoros, especially during the dry season, likened the scene to approaching an oasis amid a wasteland. It is easy to forget in our modern era of high-speed interstate highways and irrigated agriculture how immense and desolate was the expanse of untamed land between the Nueces to the Bravo, which Spaniards had long ago dubbed El Desierto Muerto. Jean Louis Berlandier noted in 1834 that the road from Matamoros to Goliad was "almost deserted" except for "some miserable huts" inhabited by those tending horses or cattle; the prairie wilderness was a "most dreadful monotony" especially after crossing the Nueces, when the landscape changed noticeably en route to Matamoros on the

Río Bravo. "No harbinger announced the proximity of that river which we avidly sought."[7]

Even approaching by sea did not readily reveal the city. "There was nothing to indicate the existence of any port or city—a bare and barren coast," wrote one seafarer, the owner of a schooner. After crossing the bar and sailing into the river, "as far as the eye could reach there seemed to exist nothing but sand plains and some scrub brushwood." One traveled half a mile before even encountering the huts at Bagdad and then sailed some three hours or more before coming in sight of Matamoros—"but there was still about fifteen miles sailing to do round by the crooked river before we reached it." Since the landscape surrounding Matamoros was fairly level, the superstructures of approaching ships could be seen from the city two or three hours before the vessel arrived, seeming to sail north, then south, only then to repeat the motion as the ship slowly wound its way on the corkscrew river, before finally arriving at a landing north of the city subsequently known as Fort Paredes, located at the Paso de la Anacuita ferry crossing.[8]

Thus to the weary traveler having crossed this wilderness, having endured the devilish chaparral, coming upon the city of Matamoros and its wild river always brought relief and even exaggerated delight. This quite naturally propelled Matamoros's growing reputation as a city of extravagant expectations. After passing some four miles from the ravine of Resaca de la Palma, "the transition was most sudden from the thick chapparal to the view of the city," wrote an astonished U.S. soldier in 1846. Another recorded, "The land on the edge of the river is, in many places, as rich as the imagination can conceive," echoing the enchantment of earlier travelers. "The city of Matamoros, viewed from the opposite side of the river, seems imbedded in the luxuriant charms of a fine level country, loaded with rich vegetation.—The first glimpse of it will always make an impression of pleasure and astonishment.... The city therefore appears buried up in a vast garden, which seems to encircle it, its houses and towers thrusting themselves up from among surrounding vegetation." Still another wrote that the closer one got to the river, the "ground appeared alive with quail, and every water hole turned out its flock of ducks." Reaching the river, the "far-famed and much-talked-about waters rolled beneath us, and the city of Matamoras rose like a fairy vision before our enraptured eyes.... No part of Texas surpasses in fertility, or equals in salubrity the Valley of the Rio Grande."[9]

Accompanying this ecstatic vision, the city's distinctive appearance echoed its growing prosperity and importance in national politics and international trade, which in turn stimulated Matamoros's great ability to stir the imagination. The main road leading into the city crossed a

Plaza de Armas, Matamoros, "bowered in trees." This illustration shows the customs house and the cathedral with its original Moroccan-style towers. *Harper's Weekly* (1866). From author's collection.

"very handsomely constructed bridge" built across a complex of estuaries (named Estero del Bravo and Estero de los Cuarteles), which one observer said "gave a semi-aquatic appearance to Matamoros and was the common resort of the inhabitants who wished to enjoy a bath." Another vision, similarly striking to a traveler emerging from the surrounding chaparral, was the charming gardens of Matamoros. "Every house except those around the public square, has a large garden attached," wrote one visitor. Another commented, "There are many fine gardens, surrounded by brick walls, in the heart of the city;—these are cultivated with taste and care,—have many flowers and shrubs . . . have many trees of orange, lemon, and lime, though china trees seem to be a favorite shade here." By 1835, the early austere homes of the founding ranching families, built mostly for defensive purposes of river sandstone and with few openings and heavy batten doors, were being replaced with brick and frame homes, many with elaborate metal balconies, even garrets, built in a variety of styles commonly described as "European" and "American," and occupied mainly by foreign merchants.[10]

The city was laid in a regular plan, the streets crossing each other at right angles. There were four public squares, three minor ones, and the

Plaza de Armas. Foreign national flags identified the English, French, American, and other consular offices in the city's center, where commercial buildings, showing North American or European architecture, symbolized the city's cosmopolitan population and ever-expanding prosperity. "The buildings, around the principal square or Plaza, are of two stories; of brick, well and handsomely built, with a fair proportion of windows; with long balconies above the lower story."[11] Appropriately, the towering Moroccan-style cathedral and neighboring customs house dominated the east side of the plaza; the municipal building and armaments (quartermaster's) building dominated the west side. As one contemporary described downtown Matamoros: "Each side of the Plaza is a solid block of buildings. On the streets leading in each direction from this, for some distance throughout the heart of the city, the buildings continue mostly of two stories, of brick; the sidewalks of the same. This part includes all the public buildings of the city, and the principal houses of business, market-house, &c. This last [the famed El Mercado], though some distance . . . of the main Plaza, is surrounded by business houses as extensive, or more so, than those around that."[12]

This scene changed as one ventured into Matamoros's suburbs. "After leaving the public square on either side, the houses decrease in size and beauty for two or three squares, when small reed and thatched huts [jacales] commence and continue to the extreme limits of the place," wrote one observer. Another similarly recorded, "On coming nearer to the exterior, the buildings are of one story, still brick, but no longer flat roofs of that material, but thatched with straw . . . When nearer still to the outskirts of the town, the brick buildings give way to cottages;—or, rather, huts;—made of cane, lashed, by strips of raw hide, to musquit poles; with roof of straw, supported by the same . . . Here, too, the sidewalks all disappear.— These cane huts occupy the larger portion of the area of the city." These dwellings also had gardens, but "are like the houses, rough; and enclosed by fences of the same light cane, fastened in the same way." The landscape then became dotted by Mexican-style thorn-bush hedge fences trussed with vines and wild flowers, which "becomes a formidable defence against a foe, defies the most viciously disposed cattle intruders, offers a shade at noon," and a home for beautiful tropical birds.[13]

But then there were also the "prevailing winds"—a regular feature of life in Matamoros, along with blowing dust, especially in dry times. One visitor, otherwise pleased with the city's appearance and hospitality, remarked that the "morning was pleasant, but the gulf breeze was very strong, and blew the dust, as we went into town, directly in our faces;— with such force were the little particles of earth and sand driven against our faces and eyes, that a continual stinging sensation was experienced;—no one could keep his eyes open a moment together." With understandable hyperbole, he exclaimed that Matamoros "has the strongest and steadiest wind, and the most of it, of any place from Maine to Yucatan. . . . In any moment, from ten o'clock each day, until sunset, the wind stops not; the dust flies along the streets in clouds, obscuring everything, . . . and every day in the dry season it is the same everlasting dust." Still, matamorenses coped. "The people have a wonderful facility in turning quickly round, to save their eyes."[14]

The winds blowing from the north proved the most perilous. As Dr. Antonio Lafon noted in his report on yellow fellow, the north winds appeared generally in October and continued until April. During, winter, even the estuaries could freeze in the cold winds; yet, the winds in the following summer could create "torrefying aridity."[15] But from October 1835 through April 1836, the north winds prevailed in ways that matamorenses could not have anticipated.

3.

PUERTA MATAMOROS: GATEWAY TO TEXAS, THE GULF ... AND THE WORLD

MATAMOROS BECAME a revenue-producing center for Mexico long before it attracted the plans of revolutionaries in Texas. Indeed, Matamoros was crucial in plans for reestablishing the Mexican economy, which had become burdened by tremendous debt incurred from the War of Independence with Spain. Matamoros would be part of the solution for keeping Texas out of the hands of expansionists from the United States by giving northeastern Mexico, including Texas, a prosperous lifestyle that patriotic and loyal Mexicans could relish. They need not look to the colossus to the north for prosperity. Even the U.S. consul in Matamoros, David Willard Smith, recognized this in an 1832 dispatch to Washington, asserting that the city had "a decided preponderance in a commercial and military point of view" to any other port on the Gulf of Mexico. (Notably, Smith was also a merchant in the city.)[1] Matamoros became *la puerta*, the gateway, to prosperity. Thus, Creed Taylor's observation that Matamoros was "an opulent city" was not the vain imaginings of Anglo Texans, but rather a reflection of both a reality and Mexican expectations already in place.

In attempting to control Texas, Mexico faced the same conundrum as had the Spanish crown: deterring aggressive Indian tribes like the Comanches and restraining American encroachment. Colonization still seemed to offer the best answer, but Mexico, like the previous royal government, faced a lack of Mexicans willing to relocate into Texas. Nevertheless, the reach of the Villas del Norte stretched wide, with Refugio (Matamoros) increasingly becoming the most important settlement among them. Economically and politically far from centers of government, the Río Bravo settlements developed an identity quite apart from that of the Mexican interior and increasingly associated themselves with Texas. Isolated on the frontier, these communities built strong trading relationships for their survival, interconnected by cart road but dependent on the flood stage of the volatile river. Even as early as 1757, the ranches of the Villas del Norte of Nuevo Santander, the Spanish province that included the present state

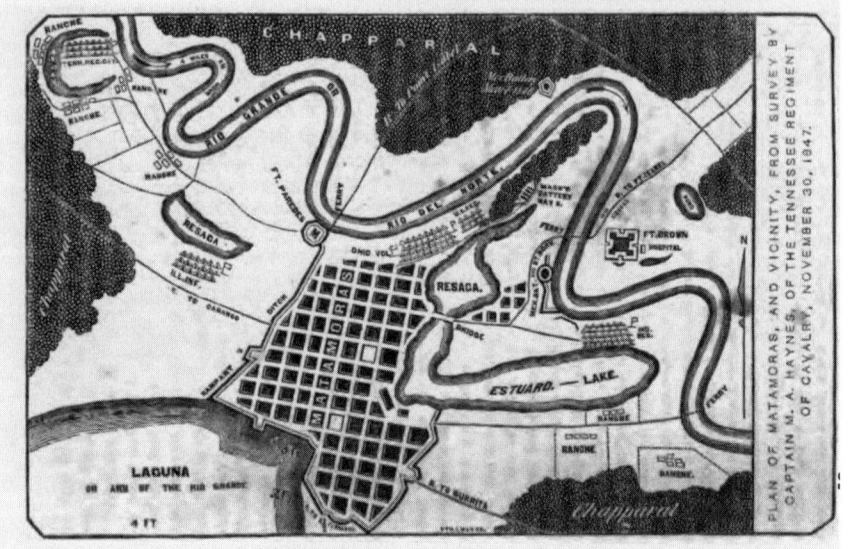

One of the earliest maps of Matamoros and vicinity, c. 1847, as surveyed by Capt. M. A. Haynes. Note the layout of the city, the fortified walls, the winding river, the ferry crossings, the lake and bridge, the chaparral, and the roads leading west to Camargo, east to Burrita (and Bagdad), and northeast to Punta de Isabel. The white square nearest the lake is the main Plaza de Armas, site of the cathedral, customs house, and municipal building. George C. Furber, *The Twelve Months Volunteer* (1848), 193. From author's collection.

of Tamaulipas and part of what is now South Texas, contained only 20 percent of the province's population but accounted for 60 percent of the *ganado mayor* (cattle, horses, mules) and 40 percent of the *ganado menor* (sheep and goats). By the end of the eighteenth century, the Villas del Norte together nearly equaled production of the haciendas and ranchos of Saltillo, which then served as the strategic economic and political hub of the northern provinces, and equaled Saltillo in tithe contributions.[2] This economic independence shaped the character of the norteños, who developed what historian David Weber called "loyalty to one's locality, one's *patria chica.*" It is no wonder that these hardy folks valued self-sufficiency, liberal principles, and local autonomy.[3]

Norteños traded livestock, hides, tallow, and wool with the haciendas and mining communities of Nuevo León in exchange for beans, wheat, corn, and cane. Such staples proved hard to cultivate because the area was prone to drought, and even the rich river bottoms were subject to the unpredictable flooding and radical course changes of the lower Río Bravo, particularly at Matamoros. La Sal Vieja and La Sal del Rey, two ancient salt lakes some fifty miles northwest of Matamoros (in present Willacy and Hidalgo Counties, Texas), supplied a valuable and seemingly inexhaustible commodity for trade—a trade even predating the Spaniards. Moreover, norteño ranchers drove herds of livestock for trade as far as Nacogdoches and points in Louisiana. Yet, despite the good quality of beef, mutton, wool, hides, salt, and even cheese and ebony, such overland commerce was both time-consuming and expensive. Spanish royal mercantilist law prohibited maritime trade except through the favored monopoly port at Veracruz, a policy that norteños believed not only kept their frontier in economic servitude and misery but also hindered other areas from benefiting from their rich resources.[4] Understandably, smuggling quickly became a respectable way of life at Refugio and the coastal hamlets of Bagdad, at the mouth of the Río Bravo, and Punta de Isabel, across from Brazos de Santiago.[5]

This economic activity, even the illegal kind, promoted growth. Refugio's 13 founding families of 1774 had become 100 families by 1800, and by 1810, the town numbered 2,000 inhabitants. By 1814, the ranchos numbered 28—more than double the original amount. By 1820, a census revealed that the population had reached 2,320 people, some having fled from upriver settlements plagued by Comanche raids.[6] The hearty spirit of these pioneer rancheros inspired them to endure isolation, marauding

Punta de Isabel (Point Isabel), established across the bay from Brazos de Santiago, served Matamoros as a much-needed deep-water port for ships too large to negotiate the Río Bravo. The hamlet was also a haven for smugglers. Thomas Bangs Thorpe, *Our Army on the Rio Grande* (1846), following p. 14. From author's collection.

Indian attacks, harsh geography, a quirky climate, and wild animals in their efforts to establish and expand their domains. Indeed, by the early 1800s, most of the vast area between the Río Bravo and Nueces had been allocated through land grants; the extensive cattle and mustang herds of these ranches roamed free, even becoming wild and adding to those herds that had long characterized the Llanos Mesteñas.[7] For example, Vicente López de Herrera, his three sons, and Gregorio Valentín Farías established Barranco Blanco ranch on the La Bahía Road at Agua Dulce Creek. Martín de León, an aristocratic *criollo* (a person born in the New World to Spanish parents) and future empresario and founder of a Mexican colony at Victoria, Texas, established a ranch between Chiltipin Creek and the Aransas River, and then a new ranch on the east bank of the Nueces River near the site of what became San Patricio. He conducted several cattle drives to market at New Orleans.[8]

As early as 1795, colonial official Félix María Calleja had recommended that the Spanish crown open a port on the Río Bravo to stimulate needed commerce in the area, a strategy first envisioned by Manuel de Escandón, son of province's founder, José de Escandón. Later, Joaquín de Arredondo, commandant-general of the Eastern Interior Provinces from 1813–21, sought to liberate the northeast from the economic monopoly of Veracruz by establishing a port at Refugio to allow trade to Havana and other seaports, an idea he shared with the "father of Mexican federalism," Miguel Ramos Arizpe, the pro-independence delegate of the Eastern Interior Provinces to the Cortes at Cádiz, the first parliament of Spain with sovereign power and a major step toward liberalism and democracy.[9] Archival sources indicate that there was a customs house at Refugio as early as 1813. But it was not until November 9, 1820, that Refugio alcalde Juan José Chapa received royal instructions by special mail: King Ferdinand VII of Spain had sanctioned the opening of Puerto del Refugio. On November 22, 1821, came even more profound news: In the final stage of Mexico's War of Independence from Spain, Pedro José García, then alcalde of Refugio, received a special courier ordered to carry out a formal ceremony of declaring independence in accordance with Agustín de Iturbide's Plan of Iguala. Refugio became part of an independent Mexican empire.

Recognizing Refugio's commercial potential, in 1823 Iturbide's new government confirmed the previous royal authorization for the port, declaring Puerto del Refugio as "essential for better communication and better trade" ("*indispensable para una mejor comunicación y un mejor comercio*"). Of course, this action legalized what had already become a very active smuggling trade, primarily with merchants in New Orleans. In 1825, the customs house was formally established, whose name, Aduana Marítima y Fronteriza del Refugio, recognized Refugio's growing importance in both maritime and frontier commerce. The supreme government's Universal Secretary of the Treasury (Secretario Universal de Hacienda) set the maritime tariff rate at a hefty 25 percent. In an effort to stimulate commerce on the river, the government also granted permission to several entrepreneurs to operate steamships on the river, first to John (Juan) Davis Bradburn and Stephen (Esteban) M. Staples, then to Henry Austin (Stephen F. Austin's cousin), whose steamboat *Ariel* made regular runs in 1829 from Matamoros to Camargo. As historian Pat Kelley notes, although their success was short-lived, other steamboats were operating on the river in 1833, 1834, and 1837. Alpheus Rackliffe, Austin's pilot, operated six American-built flatboats on the river from 1830 to 1842.[10]

The War of Independence from Spain (1810–21) had devastated the Mexican economy as farms were burned, animals slaughtered, mining equipment destroyed, commerce disrupted, and currency (capital) withdrawn from circulation or exported. Opening Refugio's port on the Bravo made strategic economic sense as part of the new nation's plan of recovery. A contemporary estimate (1817) put damages from the War of Independence at 70 million pesos for agriculture, 20 million pesos for mining, 11.8 million pesos for industry, and a whopping 786 million pesos for currency, mostly silver. To this must be added the collapse of the credit structure, already severely weakened when the Spanish crown confiscated church wealth to fund the Napoleonic wars in Europe, forcing church bodies to foreclose on loans totaling 44 million pesos—which in turn had fueled discontent in favor of independence. The economic chaos and credit collapse after independence forced Mexico's government and entrepreneurs to turn to foreign sources for credit and to seek promising streams of tax revenues such as a port at Refugio might provide.[11]

Emperor Iturbide's abdication in 1823 led to the creation of a new federal-style government in 1824. In this new republic of Mexico, the former Spanish province of Nuevo Santander became the constitutional free state (*estado libre*) of Tamaulipas.[12] In such renaming, language itself helped create new symbols for the new republic. Former Spanish viceregal rituals and public processions, such as celebrating the commemoration of the king's coronation and the king's birthday, were replaced with professions of honor to the heroes of independence and especially celebrations of September 16 (Independence Day), which symbolized federalism, education, freedom of the press, and national sovereignty. Likewise, *patria* (fatherland) and *ciudadano* (citizen) replaced the colonial *provincias* (provinces) and *subditos* (subjects). Two civic categories, ciudadano and *paisano* (countryman), replaced Spain's gradient and exhaustive racial labels.[13]

So it was in this context that on January 28, 1826, Don Lucas Fernández,

governor of Tamaulipas, authorized the decree passed by the state Constitutional Congress, which proclaimed that Refugio be elevated in status
to a villa (town) and renamed "Matamoros" to perpetuate the memory of
Mariano Matamoros, one of the exalted martyrs of the new nation. That
year the population reached 3,993, with the ranchos reporting 25,319
horses, 7,623 cattle, and 27,082 sheep and goats. The ranchos of Matamoros enjoyed a brisk and profitable business selling mules, cattle, working
oxen, and especially horses—both wild and broken—to buyers in Tamaulipas, Nuevo León, and Texas. Moreover, Matamoros quickly became
the long-awaited international maritime port and conduit of a volumi-
nous trade—now legal—for the entire northeastern region of Mexico.
Recognizing its commercial potential, merchants—Mexican, European,
and North American—flocked to the town, which blossomed to 7,000
residents by 1830. The town's increase in trade was quickly reflected in
monthly tax revenues through the customs house, which in 1826 reached
51,000 pesos, and exceeded 100,000 pesos by 1832, making Matamoros
the largest town on Mexico's northern frontier.[14] The flourishing trade at
Matamoros allowed for financial creativity in a tenuous economy, especially given that the government appropriated the revenue of the Matamoros customs house to pay the army on the northern frontier. *The
Merchants' Magazine and Commercial Review* reported that the commandant of Matamoros issued bonds against the customs house for $150,000
"receivable for all kinds of duties as cash." The merchants of Matamoros
could purchase these bonds at the rate of 3 percent interest per month
"until they had duties to pay, which they could extinguish by the drafts."[15]
These ever-increasing revenues became vital to a Mexican national government trying to pay down tremendous debts. The combined revenues
from Tampico and Matamoros also "completely financed the daily needs
of the military in northeastern Mexico."[16]

Even so, the tradition of smuggling continued to be alluring, both
to Mexican traders as well as to immigrant merchants who had settled
in Matamoros, many of whom married into prominent Mexican ciudadano families. Drawing upon their long-standing relationships with
foreign merchants, particularly at New Orleans, *contrabandistas* (smugglers)
imported clothing, shoes, liquor, tiles, corn, rice, flour, coffee, sugar, cotton,
and tobacco, and exported hides and wool, but mostly silver bullion used
to pay for smuggled imports: a "regulated system of smuggling" is how
one Englishman put it in 1826.[17] Techniques of deception included fal-
sifying documents and bribing customs house officials, using false com-
partments in ships and wagons, transferring goods to lighter vessels able
to dock at secluded areas along the coast, then hiding contraband on area
ranches and transporting the goods overland by ox cart or muleteer to

Matamoros. Although national mercantile law decreed in 1828 that all ships transporting goods to Mexican ports were to be Mexican-owned and -crewed, Americans and Europeans owned and manned most of the ships involved in the smuggling trade. On the other hand, Mexicans provided the preponderance of overland transport.[18]

Given the city's centrality to the region's trade, the time-honored oxcart driver (*boyero*) and muleteer (*arriero*) were ubiquitous on the roads to Matamoros. (A modern parallel would be the innumerable freight trucks on today's roads and highways.) "We met these continually," commented one observer in Matamoros in 1846, for "the whole internal commerce of Mexico is carried on by means of [them]." All manner of goods, supplies, and necessities were constantly being transported to the Matamoros customs house from the city's three unloading docks—at the Paso de la Anacuita ferry crossing just north of the city (subsequently known as Fort Paredes), at Bagdad near the river's mouth, and at the deep-water landing at Punta de Isabel across from Brazos de Santiago. Finally, the goods were on their way to merchant houses of Matamoros and beyond. The heavily laden transports and patiently plodding animals populated the roads to Camargo, Reynosa, Laredo, and the other northern towns, to Monterrey and Saltillo, to San Luis Potosí, Zacatecas, to faraway Chihuahua and Durango, and into Texas on the La Bahía Road. While Texas also received goods (legal and contraband) through a number of Texas ports (small ones like Copano and Linnville, but especially Galveston and Velasco), the landlocked northern Mexican states had few options other than Matamoros, Tampico, and Veracruz. Two, four, even six or more oxen pulled overloaded oxcarts (*carretas de bueyes,* or *carretas de transporte*), while a full drove of pack mules (*atajo*)—equipped with special pack saddles (*aparejos*) and attended by laborers (*peónes*)—could number even sixty animals![19]

Understandably, the commandant generals of Mexico's Eastern Interior Provinces, Manuel de Mier y Terán, Vicente Filisola, Martín Perfecto de Cos, and Pedro Lemus located their headquarters in Matamoros as the most strategic point to supervise the political and military affairs in Coahuila y Tejas, Nuevo León, and Tamaulipas. More and more professionals—merchants, shopkeepers, government officials, clerks, doctors, lawyers, teachers, craftsmen, even entertainers—were drawn to Matamoros, as were travelers and foreigners. It became increasingly common to hear English, French, Italian, German, and other languages spoken amid the dominant Spanish as the city nurtured its international and cosmopolitan character. Jews immigrated to Matamoros to escape prejudice and persecution, as did runaway slaves. Although the Mexican government abolished slavery in Mexico in 1829, it granted an exception to Texas to placate Anglo

D.ʳ MANUEL DE MIER Y TERAN.

Ministro de Guerra, de Octubre á Dbre. de 1824.

Litg. de la V. de Murguia é hijos

José Manuel de Mier y Terán, commandant general of the Eastern Interior Provinces (Coahuila y Tejas, Nuevo León, and Tamaulipas), headquartered his office in Matamoros, installed its office of collector of customs, and ordered the city's distinctive fortifications. Terán saw Matamoros as crucial for the national economy and preserving Texas for Mexico. Manuel Rivera Cambas, *Los gobernantes de México* (1873), appendix. From author's collection.

American colonists. Even so, the national government and the state legislature of Coahuila y Tejas continued to threaten the institution, causing proslavery advocates in Texas to circumvent such designs. The intent of the government was to grant free blacks full rights of citizenship, including land ownership. As early as 1831 plans were discussed to colonize fugitive slaves on the Mexican frontier, both to provide a home for them as well as to protect against the increasing Anglo American presence in Texas. Escaping to Matamoros was an attractive option for fugitive slaves despite the life-threatening obstacles of semi-desert conditions between the Nueces and Rio Grande, ignorance of the route to Mexico, slave-hunting parties, and risk of capture by Comanches or Apaches.[20]

The polyglot population gave Matamoros additional value in intelligence gathering. Col. José María Diaz Noriega, who was commissioned for a fact-finding mission by the Mexican government, was given secret instructions: "Seek with the greatest prudence all news that [you] can regarding the conduct of the Anglo American consul at that port related to the affairs in Texas."[21] Of course, it cut the other way. Colonists in Texas, notably Tejanos and Irish in San Patricio, Refugio, and Victoria, had family and friends in Matamoros who regularly supplied them with crucial information they could use against those in power in Mexico.

Some Mexican officials saw the economic development of Matamoros as a way to tie the increasingly wayward province of Texas to the rest of Mexico. "Without searching for models abroad," Simón Tadeo Ortiz de Ayala asserted to his government in 1831, look to the "flowering of Tampico, Matamoros and Mazatlan." Free trade (*comercio libre*) connecting Matamoros, Galveston, and Matagorda to other Mexican and international ports was vital. He recognized particularly that the Río Bravo del Norte, "the largest in the Republic," if developed and promoted, would serve as a "bastion and ramparts against the savages," preserve the "integrity of the national territory," and be a conduit for trade and civilization.[22]

Juan Nepomuceno Almonte prophesized in 1835 that "Texas is soon destined to be the most flourishing section of this republic," but asked rhetorically, "If, then, the condition of Texas is so prosperous what prevents Mexicans from enjoying its prosperity?" Part of the answer was "to encourage sea trade between Texas and ports of the Gulf of Mexico." He recommended allowing "coastwise trade between the colonies in Texas and the ports at Matamoros, Tampico, and Veracruz. Only thus," he stressed, "will we succeed in making the Texans build closer connections with the rest of the republic (which up to the present they ignore) and send their products to the interior." Instead, he noted with economic emphasis, the Texans preferred selling their products, especially cotton, in

New Orleans, "due to the direct connections they enjoy with that port and notwithstanding the fact they sell it there at six or eight per cent less than they would at Veracruz or Matamoros."[23]

Opening trade would also reduce smuggling, which in turn would serve to increase the relevance and value of Matamoros as the "natural center" of the region's commerce. Almonte estimated that the mostly illegal trade into Texas, primarily coming through Galveston and Matagorda, "now exceeds 600 thousand pesos annually" and predicted it would reach a million pesos within a year. Significantly, he stressed, these goods "are not all consumed within the country; they penetrate through Tamaulipas and Nuevo León into the states of San Luis Potosí, Zacatecas, Durango, and Chihuahua." Such multiregional commerce should logically be funneled through Matamoros "because since the port of Matamoros is closer to the center, it should be more natural for imports to come through there. But," he continued, "since through Texas they pay no duties whatsoever, unless a merchant wishes in good faith to send some goods through customs at Goliad—the only one that exists at the present—it follows that they find it very convenient to introduce those goods through the aforesaid [Texas] ports."[24]

In addition to transforming the local and regional economy and strengthening Matamoros's ties and importance to the national government, opening the port at Matamoros extraordinarily accelerated changes already underway in the town as social and cultural isolation rapidly diminished. In merely a few years after independence, as historian Juan Mora-Torres has emphasized, "Matamoros liberated the frontier from the center's commercial domination, forever altering center-periphery trade relations by reversing commercial roles." Indeed, he continues, "Two-thirds of all imported goods directed to the region north of Guadalajara and Querétero passed through Matamoros."[25]

Ranching, though still important in the cultural and economic life of Matamoros, now was a component of a much more elaborate society in which commerce and trade increasingly dominated. Moreover, the military became a constant presence. As military commanders repeatedly called upon matamorenses to furnish cattle and horses to their troops, grumbling increased, as did formal protests and acts of passive disobedience. Not surprisingly, political views varied, though matamorenses tended toward federalist rather than centralist views. At least eight gazettes appeared in the city, including the ultraliberal, profederalist *El Mercurio del Puerto de Matamoros*, published by the colorful George ("Jorge") Fisher, who had earlier served as customs collector, auctioneer, and official interpreter for the port Matamoros. (Fisher was conversant in more than a dozen languages.) Authorities ultimately shut down the paper and expelled Fisher for being part of the plot with José Antonio Mexía to occupy Tampico in hopes of instigating revolt against Santa Anna.[26]

Nevertheless, as David Weber observed, having broken free of the grasp of Spanish colonial mercantilism, norteños—especially matamorenses— ardently embraced American capitalism.[27] That vision was intoxicating, but it would have unanticipated and grave repercussions in Texas. Long before revolutionaries in Texas saw economic gain or alliance in Matamoros, the city was generating local, regional, and national wealth. It had become the region's commercial and military center, donning the mantle of headquarters for the Eastern Interior Provinces and was a major element in the government's strategy in preserving Texas for Mexico. The expectations were high, for much was at stake.

4.
PATRIÓTICA MATAMOROS:
REVOLUTION IN TEXAS

"Nothing will aid Texas so much as an expedition from N. Orleans against Matamoros under Gen'l Mexia. It is all important."
—Stephen F. Austin to president of the consultation,
November 5, 1835[1]

HURACAN WAS THE ANCIENT CARIBBEAN GOD of wind and storm, who visited judgment upon the earth. Spaniards transliterated the indigenous word, likely of Taíno or Carib origin, into *huracán* to describe the terribly violent storms that seasonally plagued the Gulf, the Caribbean, and the Atlantic.[2] Hurricanes were well known to peoples dwelling in the Bajo Bravo; the city of Matamoros prospered in spite of them. Perhaps it is just coincidence that the turbulent Texas Revolution was bracketed by two devastating hurricanes, each hitting Matamoros, one in 1835 and another in 1837. However much the first was prophetic, as insurrection brewed in Texas and northeastern Mexico, the second, called the "Racer's Storm," could be taken as an ominous sign that Mexico had lost Texas. It pummeled Matamoros for three days, October 2, 3, and 4, and reportedly "drove the vessels on shore and prostrated all the buildings."[3]

Historians have solidly established that the Texas Revolution started as part of a civil war between centralists and federalists within Mexico and developed into a war of independence in Texas even as the civil war continued in Mexico. This dramatic shift in Mexico occurred in 1834–35 when President Santa Anna, "El Presidente," ousted his own federalist vice president, Valentín Gómez Farías. Then Santa Anna assumed dictatorial powers—although historian Will Fowler reminds us that El Presidente's apparent pursuit of personal autocratic power is more complex and less triumphant than the traditional Texas story contends.[4] Even so, Santa Anna dissolved the "radical" Congress, installed a new centralist government and a new conservative Congress, which by "the will of the nation," rewrote the liberal Constitution of 1824 and allowed El Presidente to dis-

Antonio López de Santa Anna, wearing around his neck the Order of Guadalupe awarded to him by Emperor Augustín de Inturbide. Brantz Mayer, *Mexico; Aztec, Spanish and Republican, Vol. II* (1853), frontispiece. From author's collection.

solve state legislatures, decrease the size of state militias, and put governors directly under his control. Reactions to Santa Anna's agenda and the erosion of state autonomy were most pronounced in the far regions; revolts occurred in Zacatecas, Yucatán, Nuevo León, San Luis Potosí, Coahuila y Tejas, New Mexico, and California. To send a clear signal to all, in April 1835 Santa Anna himself, as general-in-chief, led three infantry divisions, one of cavalry, plus eighteen artillery pieces—an army of some 3,300 soldiers—to Zacatecas, where he quickly and brutally crushed the rebellion. As Fowler notes, "Santa Anna did not forgive disloyalty" and "expected his allies to remain faithful even if *he changed sides*."[5]

Federalists continued to organize but with limited success. For one significant example, General José Antonio Mexía, who was very popular among federalists in northern Mexico and Texas and enjoyed support from the United States, organized an expedition of some 160 men in New Orleans to take Tampico, a scheme that he hoped would draw upon the cooperation of federalist supporters in the city's garrison and surrounding area.[6] Ironically, in 1832, Mexía had helped Santa Anna (then a proclaimed federalist) to gain power over centralist President Bustamante by sailing with an expeditionary force from Tampico to capture Matamoros for Santa Anna. Mexía entered Matamoros without meeting resistance, the garrison having proclaimed loyalty to Santa Anna and federalism. Mexía then took his force to Brazoria in Texas, to contend with rebellions at Anahuac and Velasco. There he was satisfied with Texan claims that they had acted not as rebels for independence but as federalist sympathizers resisting local centralist commanders—though historian Josefina Zoraida Vázquez asserts that Mexía "confused Texan ambitions with the federalist struggle" and so was duped.[7]

But in 1834, when Mexía opposed Santa Anna's about-face to centralism, he was soon captured and then exiled. In New Orleans, Mexía plotted the expedition against Tampico mainly with American filibusters and with the financial backing of what historian Edward L. Miller called "confederations of merchants." These investors utilized land investments in Mexico to finance some of the most high-profile revolutionaries during this turbulent period, including Father Miguel Hidalgo y Costilla, José Bernardo Gutiérrez de Lara and Augustus W. Magee, Dr. James W. Long, and now Valentín Gómez Farías and Mexía. They also financed the New Orleans Greys, who would fight in both the Alamo and Goliad campaigns and participate in the Matamoros expedition.[8]

In the wake of Santa Anna's consolidation of power, the growing size of the centralist army garrisoned at Matamoros amplified the political rift between the city and the national government, which only intensified as hostilities erupted in Texas. As tensions mounted, local citizens reacted much as they had during Mexico's War of Independence. During that conflict, matamorenses had committed small, individual acts of passive resistance and creative noncompliance against the demands that the royal Spanish government and army had put on their community. Now, they employed more blatant tactics against Santa Anna's centralist army. With the steady arrival of these regiments on their way into Texas, the military increased its requests and then demands for matamorenses to provide provisions, livestock, money, transportation, housing, and even recruits. Tensions and complaints escalated; abuses inevitably occurred. Confrontations ensued between soldiers and residents—in bars, in fights over women and domestic servants, in civil lawsuits against soldiers for stolen property and unpaid rent. The military failed to repay loans from civilians, despite repeated requests. Warnings to matamorenses against aiding rebels in Texas in any way jeopardized their long-cultivated family, friendship, and business ties with the settlements at San Patricio, Refugio, Goliad, and Victoria.

The relationship between matamorenses and the Mexican military was not always antagonistic, however. For laborers in the Matamoros area, military service promised increased freedom and economic opportunity; likewise for female domestic servants, establishing relationships with soldiers offered the promise of escaping their local circumstances in hopes of moving elsewhere. But even these opportunities fueled conflict among the community's elite by disrupting their society and business at a time when these same elites were called upon to pay the high costs of hosting the army. As historian Omar S. Valerio-Jiménez asserts, this conflict "further distanced the town from the national government at a time when the country most needed popular support in order to put down the Texas rebellion." The *ayuntamiento* (city council) of Matamoros not only issued strong protests to the government, condemning the soldiers as "military despots," but even asked for retribution for the "harms suffered by its citizens," notably the interruption of trade, shortages of basic supplies, and outrages committed. This divisive and volatile situation is not appreciated in the traditional interpretations of the Texas Revolution, but was surely known and understood in 1836 by those colonists in Texas with connections in Matamoros. In fact, matamorenses forged an identity of "loyal resistance."[9] As their formal protests fell on deaf ears in the national government, they increasingly sought to hinder the army's efforts, even helping soldiers—chronically underpaid and undersupplied—to desert. Moreover, given that the Apache and Comanche threat was far greater for Matamoros and the other Villas del Norte than was any danger from Texas, the preoccupation of Santa Anna and his military with Texas gave further evidence that the government neither understood nor cared.

The Comanches redoubled their efforts and greatly expanded their domain in Texas and northeastern Mexico in the chaotic years following Mexican independence. They successfully created for themselves an imperial domain, not unlike the expansionary nations of Mexico and the United States. In 1833, Berlandier recorded that Comanches "launched a dreadful war" that "thoroughly devastated most of the eastern interior states," and "around Matamoros they have pushed as far as the banks of the Río Bravo, where they perpetuated a number of atrocities." Livestock herds were greatly diminished through slaughter and capture. Agriculture deteriorated as anxious farmers left their fields unattended. Indeed, the roads from Matamoros to San Patricio, Goliad, and San Antonio now crossed a "desolate and uninhabited country," Berlandier wrote. Travelers had to keep "a constant lookout for hostile Indians all the way."[10]

Seizing control of the Apache raiding trails from Matamoros to Chihuahua, the Comanches became the dominant power, despite regular assaults by the Mexican military and its Indian allies and attempts to negotiate peace. But as Mexico was facing rebellion by colonists and American intruders in Texas in 1835, the new commanding general of the Eastern Interior Provinces, Martín Perfecto de Cos, met with three hundred Comanches in August in Matamoros and managed to form a treaty. Ironically, Anglo settlers in Texas saw such efforts as a centralist plot to use the Comanches as allies against Texas—a conspiracy widely reported in newspapers in the United States.[11] Yet, at least one Matamoros newspaper judged the Comanches as no different than the "traitors" in Texas; both "violated the faith" they owed to the government, thus "violating the national honor," so neither deserved any claim to citizenship in the Mexican republic.[12] Largely because of the economic disruptions caused by military demands and Indian attacks, foreign merchants began to leave.

Despite these disruptions, Matamoros remained an attractive target to rebels in Texas, who grew more assertive by the end of 1835. By that time, Anglo American colonists vastly outnumbered Tejanos and had little desire to integrate into Mexican society. Texas had become a hotbed of racial prejudice fueled by cultural, political, and religious differences, which in turn caused Anglos and Mexicans to distrust, misread, and underestimate each other—even though they could be potential allies in the fight against Santa Anna's consolidation of power. Also, the expansionist policy of the United States emboldened Anglo American immigrants in Texas, who longed for the customs and governmental system of their home country, to rebel against Mexico. Armed volunteers like the New Orleans Greys streamed in from the United States to aid them. Their hopes were not forlorn: in the not too distant past, the United States had annexed Louisiana and Florida—Thomas Jefferson even believed that Texas should have been included in the Louisiana Purchase. Moreover, the economic importance of slavery for the colonists galvanized many Anglo Texans against Mexico's steps to limit or abolish the institution.

In November of that year, a provisional government was established by a mostly Anglo Consultation, a meeting of prominent Texans dissatisfied with the current administration in Mexico. Henry Smith served as governor and James W. Robinson as lieutenant governor. The Consultation also established a General Council, a representative body. Although the Consultation officially pledged fidelity to the Constitution of 1824, many influential Texas partisans favored independence, including Smith and Robinson.[13] Notably, the overwhelming majority of delegates who attended the Consultation were Anglo American. No delegates served from the predominately Tejano or Irish districts—Béxar, Goliad, Victoria, Refugio, or San Patricio.

Given Matamoros's geographic location, its prominent role in the Mexican government's economic strategy, its rising wealth and reputation, its fidelity to federalism, and its natural connection to the Texas settlements served by the La Bahía Road, Texans naturally thought that seizing the city could supply much needed revenue for their own efforts against Santa Anna. But it is worth reemphasizing that this Texan plot merely echoed the Matamoros policy already in practice by the national government, using the valuable proceeds from the port to pay down the national debt and finance the daily needs of the military in northeastern Mexico.

The Texan Matamoros expedition is traditionally credited to (or blamed on) Dr. James Grant and Frank W. Johnson—a charge largely due to Sam Houston's influential interpretation of the situation. Citing land speculation and defending his own actions, Houston charged that Grant and Johnson acted merely in self-interest to the near destruction of the Texas cause, which he then stepped in and saved. But the idea of attacking Matamoros actually originated with the Tejanos of the Trans-Nueces area together with the federalists of Tamaulipas and Coahuila, who were hoping to form an opposition movement commanded by the popular General Mexía. In Texas, Philip Dimmitt, who commanded a garrison of colonists at Goliad after ousting the small centralist force stationed there, proposed as early as October 15, 1835, in a letter to Stephen Austin the idea to strike out against Matamoros with the goal of persuading federalists in the interior to launch a counterrevolution against Santa Anna. Dimmitt advocated capturing the centralist Fort Lipantitlán at San Patricio as part of a plan to "give security to the frontier . . . Strike a panic and encourage the counter [federalist] revolution in the interior and if a dash were made on Matamoras the Stroke—might be followed by the most important consequence to the present and future repose of Texas."[14] As a member of De León's colony and married to María Luisa Laso, whose father, Carlos Laso, was a De León colonist and kinsman of Martín De León, Dimmitt was well connected. He maintained trade interests at Victoria and nearby Dimmitt's Landing on the coast, at Béxar, and in Zacatecas. Dimmitt estimated that Matamoros took in about $100,000 in monthly revenue, which in his opinion was much lower than it could be.

Goliad was itself the crucial hub of road systems connecting Matamoros and the other Villas del Norte to Béxar, San Felipe, the ports of Copano, Matagorda, Velasco, and even the Louisiana frontier. At Goliad, Dimmitt maintained a scouting, intelligence, and courier service, which consisted of his many Tejano and Irish contacts among colonists in the area of Victoria, Goliad, Refugio, and San Patricio, who in turn had connections in Matamoros, Camargo, Reynosa, and deeper into Mexico. Indeed, historian Hobart Huson has argued that Dimmitt probably channeled more information about Mexican plans and movements to the provisional government than any other single source.[15] In 1835, Dimmitt was convinced that a maneuver against the centralist garrison at Matamoros "would be approved and sustained by a majority of people in that section of the country." Dimmitt thought it strategically crucial that the person to lead this assault should be a *Mexican* federalist seeking to preserve the Constitution of 1824; he recommended Gen. Lorenzo de Zavala.[16]

Although Stephen F. Austin found Dimmitt's proposal attractive, he was more immediately concerned with assaulting centralist forces under Martín Perfecto de Cos now garrisoned at San Antonio de Béxar. Santa Anna had sent Cos to Texas to put down the insurrection. Like Dimmitt, Austin stressed that the Matamoros project had to be led by a native Mexican such as Mexía or Zavala to prevent charges of national or racial motivation. "Nothing will aid Texas so much as an expedition from New Orleans against Matamoros under Genl Mexia," Austin wrote; "It is *all* important." Mexía's success would help cause Cos's defeat, Austin surmised, because funds, troops, and supplies to San Antonio would be cut off. Austin also suggested that General Zavala should publicize the project in the United States, because "even a *rumor* of such a thing would keep [centralist] troops from being sent to Texas." Austin's strategy notwithstanding, Mexía was then preparing to launch an attack on Tampico instead. Zavala warned that a victorious attack on Matamoros would depend upon Mexía's success against Tampico. As late as December 9, 1835, Zavala still advised Dimmitt to launch an expedition against Matamoros, but cautioned him to do so only in the event that Mexía's maneuver against Tampico succeeded.[17]

Mexía hoped to inspire insurrection against Santa Anna in Tamaulipas, but his assault on Tampico in mid-November was emphatically crushed. Although Mexía and a remnant of his force escaped to Texas, thirty-one were taken prisoner in Tampico; three died of wounds and the rest were shot—a clear sign of Santa Anna's intent to smash federalist rebels. After Mexía's failure, the New Orleans investors lost faith in federalism and prodded rebels in Texas, including Stephen F. Austin, to support independence from Mexico and annexation to the United States.[18]

During the fall of 1835, Dimmitt pursued his plan against Matamoros. As part of this strategy, Dimmitt achieved victory against the small centralist garrison under Capt. Nicolás Rodríguez at the earthen and wood Fort Lipantitlán at San Patricio on November 3, which removed the only

José Antonio Mexía, federalist brigadier general, plotted with American financiers in New Orleans and revolutionaries in Texas to launch an expedition against Santa Anna to capture Tampico. Stephen F. Austin argued that Mexía should lead an expedition against Matamoros, but the Texan strategy soon devolved into conflicting, separate commands under Dr. James Grant and Francis W. Johnson, Sam Houston, and James Walker Fannin. John Frost, *History of Mexico and Its Wars* (1882), 171. From author's collection.

Mexía

remaining centralist fortified position between San Antonio and Matamoros. Although Dimmitt planned the exploit, his adjutant, Ira Westover, a Power and Hewetson colonist, led the actual attack, with John J. Linn, James Kerr, and James Power accompanying as advisers. Nevertheless, by mid-November 1835, Dimmitt began to doubt the commitment of federalists of interior Mexico to reestablish the Constitution of 1824. He expressed his concerns to Austin that a Texas-led attack on Matamoros "would be as likely to be opposed, as to be approved" by the citizens of northern Mexico. Moreover, Dimmitt was becoming convinced that "all of Mexico will unite in a war against Texas," persuading him that "Texas is to stand alone."[19] His concern stemmed from his learning of Mexican plans and movements through his various contacts and from the arrival at Goliad on November 11 of the federalist governor of Coahuila y Tejas, José María Viesca, and the secretary of the legislature, Dr. James Grant, who had fled his thriving hacienda in Coahuila in the wake of Santa Anna's troops.

After Santa Anna's brutal subjugation of Zacatecas, Governor Viesca and fellow radical federalists feared Santa Anna would next march into Coahuila. On May 21, 1835, the Coahuila y Tejas state legislature disbanded and authorized Governor Viesca "to establish an office in another part of the State that is not the capital." He set out for Béxar, issuing an appeal: "Citizens of Texas, arise and take arms, or sleep forever! Your most cherished interests, your liberty, your properties, even more, your very existence depend on the changing whims of your most relentless foes." Martín Perfecto de Cos arrested Viesca with Grant and others, but all escaped, thanks to the help of federalist Col. José María González. With González's assistance, Grant and Viesca made their way once again to Béxar, passing through Goliad. Historian Josefina Zoraida Vázquez asserts that Viesca "undoubtedly misinterpreted the Texan rebellion as sympathetic to the federalist cause."[20]

Nevertheless, Viesca and Grant's arrival apparently shook Dimmitt's confidence in the federalists to sustain common cause with Texas against Santa Anna. The meeting also produced hard feelings, as Dimmitt did not want to recognize the governor's authority, thereby creating an adversary in Grant, who took offense. Dimmitt's actions toward Viesca created such division and bitterness that the presidio commander felt compelled to put Goliad under martial law, which intensified the controversy. Complaints caused Austin to remove Dimmitt from command, but his men quickly informed Austin that "we esteem, we highly respect, and we love him," and therefore they had exercised their right to elect him commander again. But most of all, General Mexía's attempt to stir up insurrection in northern Mexico at Tampico in mid-November 1835, ended in disaster and defeat, which helped to convince Dimmitt, along with Houston and Smith, that a similar expedition against Matamoros would probably suffer a similar fate. Still, it did not dissuade others of notable influence. George Fisher, former customs collector of Matamoros, who had been expelled for publishing the radically pro-federalist *El Mercurio* and plotting with Mexía to occupy Tampico, still assured the General Council of the Texas provisional government (as communicated through John Power) "that in February next there is a general plan for revolutionizing all over Mexico." The only spark needed was the expedition upon Matamoros.[21]

5.

PLANNING A BRILLIANT FOLLY: THE TEXAN EXPEDITION

DESPITE HIS GROWING DOUBTS, Philip Dimmitt continued to stress the advantages of occupying Matamoros. Apparently his family and business contacts in the interior, plus a visit from Julián Pedro Miracle, representing Capt. Antonio Canales Rosillo, encouraged him enough to trust that federalist cooperation could still be forthcoming under General Mexía and others.[1] In a widely publicized letter written on December 2, and published in part in the *Texas Telegraph and Register*, Dimmitt asserted four essential points: (1) Matamoros's considerable revenues could help defray the cost of opposing Santa Anna; (2) that the occupation of the port city could possibly be used to barter peace; and (3) that through the leadership of a Mexican national such as General Zavala, a sizable force of Mexican federalists and Texans could paralyze Santa Anna's movement and even serve to launch a war to the interior of Mexico, thus (4) keeping the war out of Texas. This last point was especially attractive to Austin, who agreed with Dimmitt's assessment that "this war is not ours, although we have been compelled, in self defence, to become a party to it."[2]

Unfortunately, General Zavala declined the invitation to lead the maneuver against Matamoros, citing frail health in a letter to Dimmitt dated December 9. Still, Austin's faith in the federalists, like Dimmitt's, was renewed in early December 1835 by meetings with Miracle and Col. José María González. Miracle assured the General Council that Mexican liberals would join with Texas in the counterrevolution against Santa Anna, providing Texas did not declare independence. Ironically, federalists had tapped Miracle himself to sound out how serious Texans were in supporting their cause.[3] Historian Harbert Davenport asserted that Miracle was "Santa Anna's clever spy," and thus tempted the General Council to send an expedition to Matamoros in order to trap them.[4] Although not all scholars have accepted this assessment, Miracle would indeed assume the role of a Mexican agent later, in 1838, when he would be sent from Matamoros into the new Republic of Texas with 126 men (including 72 Mexicans, 34 soldiers, and 20 Cherokees and Caddoes) to recruit various

Texas Indian groups and Tejanos still loyal to Mexico to "take up arms in defense of the integrity of the Mexican territory in Texas" and coordinate their alliance with a campaign by the Mexican army under General Urrea to recapture Texas for Mexico.[5]

On December 8, 1835, José Antonio Fernández, the federalist governor of Tamaulipas, issued a decree that cast doubt on the possibility of an alliance between norteño federalists and the Texan rebels. Alarmed by the "need and urgency" caused by Texan schemes and actions, the governor called for the raising of a thousand troops from Tamaulipas and Nuevo León to be commanded by "our worthy compatriot" (*"nuestro digno compatriota"*), Gen. Francisco Vital Fernández, to fight against the rebel Texans—who were portrayed in opposing terms as "unworthy" or "despicable" colonists (*"los indignos colonos"*). Because these rebels had "vilely outraged" the "honor and dignity" of the Mexican republic, the governor called upon these troops—upon whom he bestowed the worthy title of "Volunteers of the Fatherland" (*"voluntarios de la Patria"*)—to "punish the audacity" of and "teach a lesson" to those "who try to attack us." This was a reference to Texas forces then besieging General Cos's garrison at Béxar as well as reports of a "Matamoros expedition" of Americans and Texans under General Mexía. Among the qualifications for these troops was a preference for those already in the militia. This rare document is significant because it was generally unknown until publicized in an auction in 2007. General Fernández, a federalist, was a presumed ally among Texans plotting an expedition to Matamoros as late as February 1836, but this decree of December 8 gives stark evidence to the contrary.[6] It would seem that even among Mexican federalists, the Texans were mistrusted.

Nevertheless, Dimmitt's letter of December 2 inspired the Texas provisional government to action. On December 17, Governor Smith ordered Houston to undertake the project, to make a "demonstration" against Matamoros, and if that failed to at least secure Goliad's port at Copano. The same day Houston, although wary of this idea since learning of Mexía's defeat at Tampico, wrote James Bowie, then at Goliad: "In obedience to the order of his excellency, Henry Smith, governor of Texas, of this date, I have the honor to direct that, in the event you can obtain the services of a sufficient number of men for the purpose, you will forthwith proceed on the route to Matamoras, and, if possible reduce the place and retain possession until further orders." Much was left to Bowie's discretion, for if nothing else, he was simply to "annoy the troops of the central army." Regardless, he was to secure the vital port of Copano, which was Houston's proposed point of debarkation. In his monumental *Three Roads to the Alamo,* William C. Davis asserts Houston's choice of Bowie was sound, for Bowie was loyal to Houston and Houston in turn trusted

Bowie's leadership and fighting skills. Nevertheless, Houston "apparently intended . . . in the end" to lead the expedition himself, while Bowie "was only to get things in motion while Houston fought the political battles raging in San Felipe." The next day, Houston sent agents to New Orleans to purchase supplies and forward them to Copano. He also ordered James C. Neill to superintend San Antonio, while William Barrett Travis and James Walker Fannin were detailed to recruit volunteers at San Felipe and Velasco respectively. Bowie left Goliad for San Antonio, however, before Houston's order reached him. Thus, the Texan Matamoros expedition, though now authorized, was still not underway.[7]

Meanwhile, Texas forces, which now included Dr. James Grant, volunteers from Goliad, Tejano companies under Juan Seguín and Plácido Benavides, and a sizable number of American volunteers, successfully stormed Cos's garrison at San Antonio during December 5–9, 1835, bringing to an end the siege of Béxar. Benavides, a son-in-law of colony founder Martín De León, was a famed militia captain, Indian fighter, and twice alcalde of Victoria; he and his band of rancheros had helped capture La Bahía (Goliad) from centralist forces in October 1835 and, at Béxar, garnered commendation for gallantry and efficiency. As it happens, Grant's friend, federalist Col. José María González, who had earlier helped Doctor Grant and Governor Viesca escape captivity, convinced two or three of Cos's cavalry units, including officers, to defect to the so-called federalist Texans.[8] The successful Texan assault forced Cos to surrender, withdraw his centralist army, and retreat to Mexico. Then, most of the Texas colonist militia went home, savoring their hard-won victory. The remnant of the "Texan" army now consisted primarily of volunteers from the United States, who became increasingly restless for more action. The volunteers elected as their new commander the peppery Francis (Frank) W. Johnson, who with Doctor Grant and Benjamin R. Milam had led the successful assault defeating Cos. (Electing officers and even voting on orders was the accepted practice in volunteer units. Such democratic excessiveness often impaired the Texan army.) Johnson organized these some 200 men, which included the New Orleans Greys, renamed the San Antonio Greys, under William G. Cooke; the Mobile Greys, originally organized by James Butler Bonham and A. C. Horton, now under David M. Burke; the United States Independent Cavalry Company from Tennessee; and the Louisville Volunteers, under James Tarleton. The latter two units were reorganized into the Kentucky Mustangs under Benjamin Lawrence.[9]

With Dr. James Grant's considerable persuasiveness, Johnson won these American volunteers over to a Matamoros expedition independent of Houston's. (Stuart Reid gives evidence that it was really Grant who was behind "old Ben" Milam's inspiring call to storm Béxar.)[10] According to

Robert C. Morris, captain of the New Orleans Greys and Grant's friend, during the siege of Béxar there had been lively talk about getting up an expedition to Matamoros, which Dr. Grant apparently inspired. This eagerness to proceed south temporarily waned as the volunteers were instead engaged in the final assault against Cos, but the zeal that Houston would later call "Matamoros rage" soon resurfaced after Béxar was taken. A campaign against Matamoros, Grant and Johnson asserted, would help retain the enthusiasm and the services of these American volunteers and adventurers, and moreover, would assist the federalist cause in northern Mexico.

Indeed, the reports that "Don Diego" Grant circulated about federalist help were encouragingly vivid, as were notions about adventure and the promise of spoils. Moreover, Grant's role in the Coahuila y Tejas legislature and his many connections, coupled with his social and economic position as a wealthy *hacendado*, gave credence to his claims. Some measure of Grant's enthusiasm is seen in his letter to Austin of November 13, 1835, written from Goliad during the earlier controversy between Dimmitt and Viesca. Grant robustly encouraged a Texas-led attack on Matamoros to aid federalist protests and uprisings that he claimed were already underway in Acapulco, Guadalajara, Puebla, Morelia, Oaxaca, and Zacatecas. Moreover, Durango, Tamaulipas, Nuevo León, and San Luis Potosí would rise in revolt "the moment an attack is made." Grant further claimed that Santa Anna's central government was "sadly distressed for funds" and its army "scattered, and cannot be united." Ultimately, "when the principles on which the freemen of Texas have taken up arms are known, i.e., the defence of the constitution of 1824, the whole republic will rise at once, and the final destruction of Santa Anna, centralism and the Spanish party [will follow] as the immediate result." In his classic history of Texas published in 1855, Henderson K. Yoakum boldly proclaimed Dr. Grant's role: "Among the volunteers and adventurers at San Antonio he was incessantly painting in lively colors the rich spoils of Tamaulipas, New Leon, Coahuila, and San Luis Potosi, the facility of the descent, the cowardly nature of the inhabitants, and the charming and beautiful valleys of the San Juan, the Sabinas, and the Santander."[11]

Nevertheless, it is significant that "Don Diego" Grant owned a large estate, Hacienda de los Hornos (Hacienda of the Furnaces) in Parras, Coahuila, now under Santa Anna's control, and was general manager of a number of haciendas in Coahuila and Zacatecas that were leased to a consortium of British companies engaged in banking and mining. His own hacienda, although cultivating wheat and containing vineyards, was primarily an industrial enterprise—hence its name—and was moving toward manufacturing cotton and wool. Moreover, the entrepreneurial Grant had partnered with John Charles Beales to settle families in the short-lived colony at Dolores on the Rio Grande. He also partnered with Johnson (as did others, such as Stephen F. Austin's associate Samuel May Williams) in buying controversial land grants issued by the Coahuila y Tejas government under duress at Monclova in the spring of 1835. (Sam Houston argued that the Texas provisional government should repudiate these land grants to avoid charges that the nascent revolution was nothing but a speculators' war.) Together with his role as a legislator, these interests guaranteed that he had a dramatic personal interest in promoting the expedition to Matamoros and encouraging the federalist cause.[12] In his lively memoir, the dauntless John J. Linn of Victoria, who knew Grant and the situation in San Antonio as well as anyone, captured perhaps the most realistic assessment. Linn characterized Grant as "a gentleman of a thorough education, elegant manners, and at his home in Coahuila, he lived like a lord and entertained like a prince." Moreover, "Dr. Grant, who doubtless sighed for the possession of his princely estates near Parras, was the soul of these schemes [against Matamoros], albeit he had ready listeners, and not a few who were ready to embark in any enterprise that possessed the elements of adventure, notoriety, and booty." Linn judged Grant's actions as purely self-interest, having "nothing particularly in common with Texas," but rather "actuated by a desire for the reclamation of his magnificent estates, and not by patriotism, as some others were."[13]

With the volunteers at Béxar now inspired to join this expedition to Matamoros, Johnson left Grant with the men, then traveled to San Felipe in order to seek formal authority from the provisional government as well as to procure funds, commissions for officers, munitions, and supplies. Indeed, the General Council, which was becoming impatient with Houston's apparent slackness in carrying out Governor Smith's order for a "demonstration" against Matamoros, welcomed Johnson—more or less. Johnson walked right into intense political squabbling between Governor Smith and the General Council under Lt. Gov. James Robinson, which soon rendered the provisional government perilously ineffective. Some insight into the situation among the volunteers at San Antonio regarding the trek to the Rio Grande is revealed in a letter from Johnson to the General Council on January 7, 1836. Johnson noted that he "yielded to [the volunteers'] desires and ordered a march on Matemoros." Quite defensively Johnson asserted, "In this as in all other acts of my public life I had solely the interests of the Country at heart and was unwilling that Matemoros should be taken until I had commissions from your body for the officers—I considered that with commissions from your body—their acts would be those of Texas and the army subject to your orders."[14]

But even as Dimmitt, Houston, and others began to doubt the dependability of the federalists—ironic, given that Mexican federalists now also saw Texans as untrustworthy—Austin astutely characterized the danger of leading an army primarily of adventurers and volunteers from the United States to Matamoros as a hugely risky venture, even under the banner of federalism and the Constitution of 1824. Indeed, before resigning his command to leave Texas as a commissioner to the United States, General Austin had issued warnings to both Johnson and the General Council about the dangers of a Texas-led expedition of "foreigners" (volunteers from the United States) to Matamoros. "Every possible aid should be given to the Federal party in the interior; but should be done as auxiliary aid . . . By doing this the war will be kept out of Texas." Austin greatly stressed that "not to do anything that will compel the Federal party to turn against us, and if they call on us for aid let it be given as *auxiliary aid*, and on no other footing." Austin's reasoning was compelling: "This takes away the character of a national war, which the government in Mexico is trying to give it, and it will also give to Texas just claims on the Federal party, for remuneration out of the proceeds of the Custom Houses of Matamoros and Tampico, for our expenses in furnishing the *auxiliary aid*. But if Texas sends an *invading* force of foreign [American] troops against Matamoros, it will change the whole matter. Gen. Mexia ought to have commanded the expedition to Matamoros and only waited to be asked by the Provisional Government to do so."[15]

But Johnson's rosy opinion of a Matamoros campaign, which Doctor Grant greatly informed, differed sharply from the doubt that Austin, Houston, Dimmitt, and others increasingly came to hold. "We can calculate with certainty on our liberals," Johnson informed Lieutenant Governor Robinson about the federalists and the citizens of Matamoros rising up against Santa Anna, presumably echoing Grant's privileged intelligence from his contacts and informants. Such an expedition would have "every rational prospect of success," Johnson stressed. "The moment is appropriate and should not be lost . . . if we are not interfered with by the officers of the regular army"—a jab at Houston—"you may rely on all going well." Grant and Johnson also launched a concerted effort to remove the outspoken Dimmitt from command at Goliad, a campaign that stemmed from personal dislike, Dimmitt's ambivalence about attacking Matamoros, his allegiance to Houston as commander-in-chief, and his alleged ill-treatment of Doctor Grant and Governor Viesca during their earlier passage through Goliad en route to San Felipe following the collapse of the Monclova government.[16]

Yet Dimmitt had his reasons, not the least of which was the disturbing testimony recently discovered by historian Thomas Ricks Lindley of his fellow De León colonists Fernando De León and José María Carbajal and his father-in-law, Carlos Laso, who had been onboard the *Hannah Elizabeth*, an American schooner bearing supplies and volunteers from New Orleans for the Texas cause. The schooner ran aground on a sandbar in Matagorda Bay and was captured by a Mexican naval vessel. De León, Carbajal, Laso, and others were captured and eventually imprisoned in Matamoros, only to escape with the help of friends and make their way back to Victoria, passing first through Goliad. They reported to Dimmitt that "on their departure they were informed by a friend that there was in circulation a Decree of the general Government That all Mexicans, foreigners, or Americans, without any distinction whatever taken as prisoners on this side of the Rio Grande should be immediately put to death." Another friend, who provided the men with horses for their escape, warned them to avoid the main road, where he saw the bodies of five "foreigners" apparently executed in accordance with the decree. De León and Laso further reported news from the commander of Matamoros's deep-water port at Brazos Santiago, who told them that the government had ordered "all vessels from N. Orleans bound to any port of Texas should be taken into Vera cruz as a Lawful Prize," and further, that five schooners were ready to sail from Veracruz to patrol the Texas coast. Even more ominously, "a courier Extra ordinary" informed them that some three thousand soldiers under General Joaquín Ramírez y Sesma, bearing also three pieces of heavy artillery, were leaving Saltillo and marching into Texas.[17]

Learning this information cinched Dimmitt's decision only two days later to take the next radical step, which history remembers as the Goliad Declaration of Independence. Given his strong family and business ties with Tejanos and Mexicans, Dimmitt's seemingly inexplicable and swift about-face from being an ardent supporter of Mexican federalism to an impassioned leader of Texas independence has long perplexed historians. Lindley, in bringing the De León-Laso report to light, offers the most plausible explanation.[18]

Nonetheless, while Johnson had gone to San Felipe to gain the council's authority for the expedition to Matamoros, Grant promptly proclaimed himself "Acting Commander-in-Chief of the Federal Volunteer Army of Texas" and—as the traditional story goes—"stripped" the supplies, medicines, arms, and equipment that Col. James Neill had painstakingly accumulated in San Antonio, thus leaving the Alamo virtually defenseless and destitute. Historian Stuart Reid calls this accusation Neill's "famous jeremiad of January 6" and provides evidence that Neill's claim was not only exaggerated but that there just were not that many supplies to take—as confirmed by Houston's comment later, when seeing these volunteers at Goliad, that they "were destitute of many supplies necessary" to carry out their Matamoros campaign. At any rate, about Christmas Eve 1835, federalist Colonel González and his men (including the defectors from General Cos) and Victoria's Capt. Plácido Benavides and his mounted company of Victoria rancheros left "to scour the countryside" and gather intelligence between the Nueces and the Rio Grande—essentially "home territory" to Benavides, a native of the Villas del Norte town of Reynosa. On December 30, Grant followed with the rest of the volunteers, despite Neill's protests.[19]

Significantly, only on January 3, 1836, did Johnson petition the council to authorize the expedition that Grant had already launched, requesting also a commission for Grant as (only) a colonel.[20] Although Johnson claimed that he had ordered the expedition himself, Grant's persuasiveness is unquestionable, especially given his self-appointed command and his personal influence on the volunteers, making Johnson's comment that he (Johnson) "yielded to the desires" of the men even more revelatory. Stuart Reid credits Grant as being the kingpin, concluding that Johnson's personal motives were "at best uncertain" and his wavering indicative of his lack "of genuine conviction."[21] Moreover, given that spoils, plunder, and land speculation were persistently rumored at the time, personal ambition cannot be ruled out—notwithstanding the role of Johnson's longtime adversary, Sam Houston, in perpetuating these rumors.

However controversial were Grant's self-appointed command, the seizure of provisions, and the departure of the volunteers from San Antonio, the long-debated Texan Matamoros expedition was indeed underway—though purposefully separated from Houston's efforts and, given the state of the provisional government, arguably without authority and under questionable intent. Henry Millard, then a member of the General Council who later distinguished himself at San Jacinto, offered valuable insight into the ultimate goal of Grant and Johnson's enterprise. Their expedition, Millard asserted in a letter of January 14, 1836, was to remain an independent force not subject to any officer appointed by the provisional government (unless they chose to be), meet with allies in northern Mexico, and form a new republic separate from Mexico—a plan, Millard claimed, that "suited well the great land speculators."[22]

En route to the Nueces River and San Patricio, where Johnson and Grant agreed to mobilize before the final push to the Rio Grande, Grant passed through Goliad. At Presidio La Bahía, he claimed superior rank over Philip Dimmitt, then commandeered the precious stores, arms, and horses that Dimmitt's garrison had painstakingly gathered, much of which was private property belonging to the residents in the Goliad and Victoria area. Grant's actions increased the existing antagonism between the two men, which stemmed from Dimmitt's earlier treatment of Governor

Viesca, his growing doubts about Mexican federalist support, and his no longer advocating an expedition to Matamoros. Dimmitt's men, who, as a force of independent volunteers (most being colonists from the Lavaca, Matagorda, and Victoria areas) were not subject to Grant's command, understandably resented Grant's seeming self-importance. Dimmitt was further incensed by Grant's questionable authority for carrying out the campaign that he himself had once promoted but now found ill advised.[23]

The discord between the two men, which grew increasingly tense, was complicated still further by actions that had already occurred at Presidio La Bahía earlier in December. His growing doubts and fears were confirmed by Fernando De León and Carlos Laso's ominous report, Dimmitt shifted to advocating complete separation of Texas from Mexico. To this end, he designed what has been called the first Texas flag of independence—decorated with a bloody arm holding a bloody sword on a white field—and raised it on December 20 to commemorate the declaration that he and Ira Westover had framed. This was not the first flag Dimmitt designed. Earlier, he had created the famous tricolor flag, based on the Mexican national flag but in place of the eagle was emblazoned the date "1824" to show loyalty to the federalist constitution. This flag may have been carried to the assault on Béxar in December 1835 and is still popularly thought to be the flag flown in the battle of the Alamo in 1836—an erroneous supposition, as the Alamo defenders were clearly fighting for independence.[24] The volunteers at the Alamo purporting loyalty to the constitution would have left with Grant—taking the 1824 flag with them. Indeed, a proclamation published in the *Texas Telegraph and Register* on January 16, 1836, and bearing the name and signature of none other than Francis W. Johnson, declared, "Under sanction of the general council of Texas, [the Federal Volunteer Army has] taken up the line of march for the country west of the Rio Grande. They march under the flag 1.8.2.4 . . . and have for their object the restoration of the principles of the constitution, and the extermination of the last vestige of despotism from Mexican soil."[25]

Dimmitt and Westover's Goliad Declaration of Independence proclaimed Texas "a free, sovereign and independent State," promising "equal, impartial, and indiscriminate protection to all; to the low and the high, the humble and the well-born, the poor and the rich, the ignorant and the educated, the simple and the shrewd." But the Mexican central government was not the only "enemy." Significantly, the document also condemned the Texas General Council's ineptitude, calling for political, if not moral, "renovation."[26] On the altar in the La Bahía presidio chapel—this is no small point—ninety-two signers ratified the document, most being area Anglo and Irish colonists, though two were Tejanos: José Miguel

Aldrete, a De León son-in-law and alcalde of Goliad, and "M. Carbajal," likely Mariano, brother of José María Carbajal, one of the men who had brought Dimmitt the ominous news out of Matamoros only two days earlier. Clearly, the declaration dramatically hardened Dimmitt's doubts about the trustworthiness of Mexicans and even reflected his attitude toward local Hispanic citizens of Goliad (*labadeños*). Dimmitt's actions to fortify Presidio La Bahía and gather beef, corn, supplies, and transport for the Texas army in Béxar during November and December 1835 caused most area Tejanos to flee to the countryside, many taking refuge at the nearby rancho of Carlos de la Garza. John J. Linn wrote to Austin protesting Dimmitt's "acts of tireney [tyranny]," which included impressing labadeños into manual labor without compensation; "they do not want to be made hewers of wood and Drawers of water," Linn wrote—which as it happens, is a direct quote from the Bible (Joshua 9:21, 23, 27 KVJ) regarding Joshua's enslavement of the Gideonites in exchange for not killing them because of their deceit—an ironic, if subtle rebuke on Linn's part.[27]

The polemical Goliad declaration would be printed and widely distributed. But the General Council, now vested in Grant and Johnson's Matamoros expedition, was naturally incensed at the Goliad document's assertions and its indictment of the provisional government. Fearing the loss of cooperation with Mexican federalists, the council criticized the document as premature and filed the original document, even suppressing further action.[28] Of course only months later, the newly formed convention at Washington-on-the-Brazos, which emerged from the dysfunctional ashes of the provisional government, would indeed issue an official declaration of independence on March 2, 1836. But this was yet to come. When Grant arrived at Goliad, the self-appointed "commander-in-chief" and representative of the council believed Dimmitt's controversial actions needed constraining for the sake of the federalist cause.

Thus Grant, touting his command and proclaiming loyalty to the Constitution of 1824 and the Texas General Council, demanded under threat of force that Dimmitt lower the "bloody-arm" flag of independence now flying over the presidio. William G. Cooke, commander of the San Antonio Greys, one of the units that had trekked from San Antonio under Grant, commented on the explosiveness of the situation: "Col. Grant, and we all expected to have a fight with his [Dimmitt's] forces"; throughout the encounter "both parties were kept in readiness for a fight." These actions caused Dimmitt to resign his command in protest about January 10, 1836, leaving the presidio in command of Capt. Peyton S. Wyatt. A courier bearing Dimmitt's protest to Governor Smith encountered James Bowie, who, having finally received Houston's orders, was en route to Goliad to take command of the Matamoros expedition. "Some dark scheme has been set on foot to disgrace our noble cause," Bowie quickly wrote to Houston. "I . . . shall reach Goliad by daylight, and put a stop to Grant's movements." But by then Grant had left Goliad with a segment of his command for Refugio, where Johnson was to join the expedition after having gained authority—for what it was worth—from the council.[29]

6.

JUDAS, SCOUNDRELS, WOLVES, AND RASCALLY ACQUIREMENTS

As THE MATAMOROS EXPEDITION was getting underway, the polemical division in the Texas provisional government flared into white heat between Governor Smith, who advocated independence, and the majority of the General Council, who still favored the federalist Constitution of 1824. Smith, who had authorized Houston to command an expedition to Matamoros, objected to Johnson and Grant's leadership because he distrusted both their motives and allegiance. His misgivings were based partially on the rumor that the two men were attempting to join with Mexican insurrectionists to establish a republic in northern Mexico that would be independent of both Mexico and Texas, an objective that was apparently no secret to Austin, Houston, or Dimmitt. If indeed this was the true goal, then it ran counter to the designs of either the independence faction or those claiming loyalty to the Constitution of 1824. Smith, like Dimmitt, also distrusted the glowing reports from the Mexican interior indicating that Mexican federalists were ready to unite in strength with Texans in a Matamoros campaign.[1]

Nonetheless, the General Council overrode Smith's opposition and on January 14, 1836, authorized Johnson's command of the Matamoros expedition now underway by Grant. Yet, in their determination to carry out the project, the council on January 7 had already appointed James Walker Fannin as "agent" of a volunteer expedition to Matamoros, authorized him to call on the prestigious merchant firm of McKinney, Williams, and Company for provisions, transportation, and munitions, and sanctioned him to recruit and assign positions as needed. As the council's agent, Fannin was essentially answerable only to himself—not the commander-in-chief or the governor—making his powers quite extraordinary.

In effect, the council issued two separate commands, one to Fannin and one to Johnson, for a Matamoros campaign independent of Houston and Smith. Although the council's intention seems to have been to respect Fannin's earlier appointment, both Fannin and Johnson recruited volunteers independently for an increasingly controversial expedition that

James Walker Fannin was one of three rival commanders (along with Sam Houston and Francis W. Johnson) appointed by the Texas provisional government to lead expeditions against Matamoros. Fannin's forces, primarily American volunteers, were defeated by Gen. José de Urrea's army and were executed in the Goliad Massacre. Portrait alleged to be of James W. Fannin attributed to his cousin, Samuel F. B. Morse. *Courtesy Dallas Historical Society*. Used by permission.

including Houston, who in turn has passed his authority on to James Bowie, now had three commanders—four, if counting Grant. Complicating things further, in a deliberate move to undermine Houston and Smith's authority, the council issued a proclamation that because Bowie held no commission in the army, which was correct, he therefore had no authority to receive orders from Houston or lead volunteers. "Ironically," writes William C. Davis, "the one Texian who to date had seen more action in independent command than any other held no official rank whatever." When John A. Wharton, one of the military agents sent to New Orleans to collect provisions, arrived at Velasco with supplies on January 30, Fannin requested they be sent to one place, while Houston directed them to another. The exasperated Wharton wrote, "I perceive that there are more commanders-in-chief than one."[2]

Houston had sided with Neill regarding Grant's earlier actions at San Antonio. He also believed that the General Council had exceeded its power by sanctioning a Matamoros expedition at all—especially one at odds with his own charge from Governor Smith. He was concerned about reports (which were true) that Santa Anna had ordered troops toward Matamoros. But Houston's motivations are cloudy. In perceiving that Johnson, Grant, and even Fannin were usurping his authority as commander-in-chief, he sought to salvage his position and reputation. In effect, he helped stir Governor Smith into attempting to dissolve the council on January 9 and 10—as it happens, during the same time that Dimmitt resigned his Goliad command in protest of Grant's actions and Johnson issued his bombastic "Proclamation of the Federal Volunteer Army of Texas," casting for American and Mexican volunteers to join the Matamoros campaign already afoot.[3] Smith called the council's dissident members "Judas," "parricides," "scoundrels," and "wolves" among the flock. The infuriated councilmen retaliated by impeaching the governor and recognizing Lieutenant Governor Robinson as the acting executive.[4]

Soon Fannin was drawn into this fray between the governor and the council. Within the space of one week, Fannin was made agent of the council for the Matamoros campaign, then Johnson was granted similar authority. Which man had preference? What about Grant? With Bowie's authority now "discredited," what about Houston?[5] In time the controversy also involved William Ward, leader of the Georgia Battalion and Fannin's second in command, with the result that these two men became embittered with each other—a situation bearing on Fannin's later tragic campaign against General Urrea's Mexican army. Governor Smith admonished Ward that Johnson and Grant were "using every exertion, to get an expedition fitted out to suit their own purposes"—intentions that included safeguarding apparent land speculation, which Smith branded "rascally acquirements." Furthermore, he warned Ward not to trust anyone trying to supersede Houston as commander-in-chief, which of course included Fannin, the council's "agent" for the Matamoros campaign. Although Ward and the Georgia Battalion still joined Fannin's command, the controversy created a rift between the two men.[6]

Thus the Matamoros project, having once inspired a viable strategy allying Texan and Mexican federalists to preserve the Constitution of 1824 against Santa Anna, now incited division and chaos in Texas, even raising doubts about Mexican trustworthiness. Governor Smith refused to resign, and the General Council, torn by strife and the exodus of its members, ceased to have a quorum after January 18. This left Texas without governmental leadership (or perhaps too much) during the crucial months of January and February 1836, when Grant and Johnson's Matamoros crusade was already underway, Neill (and then Travis) called for volunteers to defend the Alamo, Fannin recruited for his own Matamoros campaign, and Houston sought to redeem his waning leadership and reputation.

Sam Houston attempted to resolve the developing crisis with a personal appearance to Grant's volunteers as they proceeded to Goliad and Refugio en route to San Patricio and Matamoros. According to a report Houston sent to Smith on January 30, on the morning of January 14, 1836, he encountered Dimmitt who, having resigned his command, had already departed Goliad with a small band of men. Dimmitt informed Houston of Grant's volatile actions. Upon entering Goliad's Presidio La Bahía later that night, Houston was surprised to find Bowie, who had arrived on January 11 bearing Houston's earlier orders to take command of the Matamoros volunteers—but Grant had already left Goliad, heading south to make contact with Colonel González's cavalrymen. Houston found the Goliad garrison, now under Peyton S. Wyatt's command (in Dimmitt's absence), on the verge of hostilities with Grant's men, who were now temporarily under recently promoted Maj. Robert C. Morris, who had refused to recognize Bowie's authority.[7]

On January 17, Houston received an urgent message from Neill at the Alamo calling for reinforcements and reporting intelligence that one thousand Mexican soldiers were marching to Béxar and two thousand to Matamoros. In response, Houston sent Bowie—perhaps Houston's only ally at Goliad—to San Antonio with about thirty other men with orders (bearing ultimately on Neill's discretion) to destroy the Alamo and retreat with the artillery to Gonzales.[8] Houston also rushed a courier to overtake Dimmitt with orders to raise a force to relieve San Antonio as well (or, if finding the Alamo abandoned, retreat to Gonzales). Although Houston claimed a desire to proceed to San Antonio himself, he asserted that dealing with the Matamoros expedition was the more immediate concern. "I would myself have marched to Bexar but the Matamoras rage is up so high that I must see Colonel [William] Ward's men," Houston wrote Governor Smith from Goliad on January 17. "You have no idea of the difficulties I have encountered." [9] Houston was anxious to get to Ward's newly arrived Georgia Battalion, which was thought to be at Refugio in order to remove this sizable force from the Matamoros campaign and send them to San Antonio or Gonzales. Houston decided that the Matamoros expedition was the paramount issue because it involved most of the Texas army yet was divisive and, as he increasingly asserted, foolhardy and calamitous. This explains in part his absence at San Antonio when crucial decisions were being made that would result in Travis and Bowie taking a stand at the Alamo—and why he would so vigorously blame "Matamoros rage" as the ultimate scapegoat in the Texas Revolution.

Despite Houston's presence, Grant's spirited volunteers continued the march to Refugio as planned, where they were to reunite with Grant's advance party, meet Johnson, be supplied from Copano, and be reinforced by Fannin's recruits, primarily Ward's Georgia Battalion. As historian Stephen Hardin astutely observes, Houston simply lacked credibility. "He may have had Smith's trust, but where had Houston been at Gonzales, at Concepción, at the Grass Fight, at the storming of Béxar? They [the volunteers] had actually seen Grant fight and bleed for the cause. To them, Houston seemed a mere poseur."[10] Based on historians' errors and supposed "lost" documents, it has long been assumed that Houston addressed the volunteers first at Goliad and again at Refugio.[11] But James E. Crisp has shown that Houston gave *both* speeches at Refugio—the Goliad speech is apocryphal.[12] So, leaving Wyatt in command at Goliad, Houston simply chose to proceed with the volunteers to Refugio—and there he would attempt to gain their confidence, establish his authority, and stop the expedition.

Of course in so doing, Houston would also attempt to salvage his own credibility. Indeed, in a letter to Smith on January 17, he credited himself with the relocation: "I will take up the line of march for Refugio Mission with about 209 efficient men, where I will await orders from your Excellency," and in light of Neill's intelligence and his own distrust, he added, "The army should not advance with a small force on Matamoros in the hope or belief that the Mexicans will cooperate with us." Arriving at Refugio, he found neither Fannin nor Ward, but they were not yet at Copano. Houston ordered about thirty regular troops already there back to Goliad, stressing that Presidio La Bahía had to be maintained to protect Copano and the crucial supply route to San Antonio.[13] While waiting at Refugio for Ward and Fannin, Houston confronted Johnson, who arrived from San Felipe on the evening of January 20, bearing his and Fannin's authorizations from the General Council. Houston was shocked and angered, both by the authorizations themselves, which he considered to have been issued illegally, and by the realization that the council overrode his own authority as commanding general. Moreover, he considered

Fannin's powers as agent of the council to be as extensive as Santa Anna's and just as much at variance with the "organic law."[14]

Houston was in a quandary. He now claimed very serious doubts about any federalist help coming from the northern provinces. As he put it, "I have no confidence in the [Mexican federalists] and the disaster at Tampico should teach us a lesson."[15] Without such help, he knew that Johnson, Grant, and Fannin's campaigns to Matamoros—which, he emphasized to Smith, was not only illegitimate but divided in command—would end in terrible defeat, especially in light of Neill's report that they would face a centralist army of two thousand men. Houston was also fearful of the repercussions of Fannin's recruitment policy, which had included the proclamation that the volunteer force should "be paid of the first spoils taken from the enemy" at Matamoros. Such action, Houston would write to Smith in his extensive and polemical missive of January 30, "divests the campaign of any character save that of a piratical or predatory war." As Houston saw it, this would naturally cause the Matamoros population—originally portrayed as supportive of an expedition—to see their situation as desperate, thus turning them into enemies. Furthermore, as he put it rather accurately, "In war, when spoil is the object, friends and enemies share one common destiny. This rule will govern the citizens of Matamoros in their conclusions and render their resistance desperate. . . . They will look upon them [Grant's volunteers] as they would upon Mexican mercenaries, and resist them as such." Furthermore, "A city containing twelve thousand souls will not be taken by a handful of men who have marched twenty-two days without bread-stuffs, or necessary supplies for an army. If there ever was a time when Matamoras could have been taken by a few men," Houston concluded, "that time has passed by."[16] Houston was exactly right: By January 31, General Urrea would occupy Matamoros and successfully draw many federalist rancheros as allies to his campaign against the rebels in Texas.

At Refugio, Houston took advantage of Grant's absence and attempted to convey his concerns to the headstrong U.S. volunteers increasingly eager for action. In his first address to the men, he was initially greeted as an outsider and confronted their displeasure, which included a rebuttal by Captain Thomas K. Pearson, who ably defended Grant and Johnson. Houston then made a desperate and impassioned second speech. Hermann Ehrenberg later recalled that Houston praised the men's courage but pleaded with them to avoid certain disaster by waiting to attack Santa Anna's army within the borders of Texas "after long marches and other hardships have exhausted and demoralized them." He also warned them that the needed support from the Mexican federalists was simply and profoundly not materializing. Of course, the federalists increasingly distrusted the Texas cause as no longer compatible with their own, especially given the involvement of so many Americans.[17]

It is noteworthy that in addition to giving this passionate oration, Houston also tried to persuade the men individually. According to witness Reuben R. Brown, the general "was constantly engaged in private conversations with the volunteers endeavoring to influence them to abandon the enterprise in which they were engaged." As Stephen Hardin rightly asserts about Houston, "He had not trained under Andrew Jackson without acquiring the ability to win a crowd." In the end, Ehrenberg stressed that "cheers of joy greeted his eloquent appeal" and Capt. William G. Cooke recorded that Houston "completely defeated the object of Col. Grant." Houston apparently managed to convince more than half of the 200 men to at least wait at Refugio for Fannin's and Ward's reinforcements, but he failed to win control of the army for himself. Not only had Johnson's authorization from the council undermined Houston, but Stuart Reid provides evidence that Grant likely returned and confronted Houston and regained command of at least sixty-four men—many veterans of Grant's leadership in the storming of Béxar—who would continue the expedition southward to Matamoros.[18]

Houston realized that because his own authority had been undermined by the General Council's sanction of both Johnson's and Fannin's commands as well as by Grant's persuasive return, his continued presence would merely serve his adversaries. As he put it, "the council would have had the pleasure of ascribing to me the evils which their own conduct and acts will, in all probability produce." Therefore, somewhat despairing of the Texas cause, he left the army and headed for San Felipe to see Governor Smith, who, on January 28, granted him furlough until March 1 to help check the dissent directed against him for his opposition to the Matamoros campaign. In a strategic roundabout, Houston would soon marshal a campaign to use the Matamoros expedition as the all-inclusive scapegoat for his own woes, which he conflated with the tribulations of the Texas cause. He utilized his furlough in part to persuade the upcoming convention meeting in March at Washington-on-the-Brazos to grant him indisputable authority over all Texas troops and to negotiate a treaty of neutrality with Texas Cherokee and related tribes, who, he argued, might be persuaded to join the Mexican side. While historians often dismiss Houston's action, there was merit to his concern, as proven later with Julián Pedro Miracle's mission in 1838 to recruit Cherokees and other Texas tribes to coordinate with the Mexican army to reconquer Texas. Meanwhile at Refugio, the recalcitrant Johnson and Grant gathered the sixty to seventy men still not swayed by Houston's pleadings and headed south for San Patricio. They were still apparently convinced that Mat-

One of the earliest illustrations of Matamoros, c. 1848, shows the city from the north side of the Río Bravo as it would have appeared to travelers coming from Texas across the Trans-Nueces Wild Horse Desert—El Desierto Muerto. Note the skyline, the ships able to navigate the tortuous river, and the ferry-type boats to cross the river. Tinted lithograph by John Phillips and Alfred Rider, *Mexico Illustrated, in Twenty-Six Drawings by John Phillips and A. Rider with descriptive Letterpress in English and Spanish* (1848), plate 26. From author's collection.

amoros was "entirely defenceless" and that federalist—and Fannin's—aid would be forthcoming.[19]

The strife and division that Johnson and Grant's expedition produced, especially in the provisional government, was underscored by a meeting on January 26 of concerned citizens and soldiers still in Béxar. Among those present were Neill, who chaired the meeting, Bowie, James Bonham, Juan N. Seguin, Green Jameson, and Don Gaspar Flores. The committee drew up resolutions condemning the actions of the General Council toward Governor Smith, especially regarding the Matamoros expedition, which they declared should have come under the authority of General Houston as "commander in Chief of all the land forces in the service of Texas." The committee pledged its support to Smith, condemning "the illegal appointments of agents and officers" made by the council "in relation to the Matamoros Expedition." Further, they denounced Grant's attempted usurpation of Houston's command, the council's misappropriation of money donated for Béxar, and the "private and designing men" of the council who sought to reopen the land offices in order to continue speculating while braver men risked their lives in the field. Ultimately, the committee condemned the council as "in the highest degree criminal and unjust," passionately denouncing its acts as "anarchical assumptions of power to which we will not submit."[20] Dishonesty, deceit, schism, strife, generating rebellion within revolution—all became characteristic of "Matamoros rage." Sadly, calamity was never far behind.

While the Texas provisional government squabbled and disintegrated, decisions were made to defend Béxar, Johnson and Grant proceeded with their plans, and Fannin successfully recruited a sizable force for his own expedition to Matamoros, as the General Council had authorized. He sailed from Velasco on January 24, 1836, and landed at Copano on February 2, with about 200 men, including William Ward's Georgia Battalion. On February 4 and 5, he marched out to join the volunteers inspired by Houston to wait at Refugio, from where, as Fannin wrote, "we will take up the line of march for Rio Grande." The expectation of forthcoming federalist support was underscored in Fannin's hopeful letter to Lieutenant Governor Robinson on February 4, in which he quoted Johnson's own encouraging words of February 2: "'Our friends, the liberals of Tamaulipas, are arriving in all quarters, and will form a most respectable addition to our force—Every thing looks most propitious, and unless our head strong countrymen, by a premature Decleration of Independence [a dig at Dimmitt's actions and those supporting Governor Smith], rouse the jealousy of the Federal party victory is secured and by one blow, we may calculate over throwing the Tyrant, Santa Anna & his minions.'"[21] However unduly optimistic Johnson and Fannin may have been, their letters at least still recognized that federalist support depended in large degree on the Texan goal—or at least the federalist perception of it—to stay loyal to the Constitution of 1824 and not to declare for independence. Nevertheless, patriotic federalists, who certainly were now aware of the Goliad Declaration of Independence, grew understandably distrustful of Texan motives—especially because the majority of the Texas army, including those in the Matamoros expedition, were volunteers recruited from the United States.

For specific evidence, Johnson claimed that their federalist allies, Col. José María González and Capt. Antonio Canales Rosillo (later nicknamed "Chaparral Fox"), awaited with 350 men; in addition there was "the certain assistance we will receive from all parts of Tamaulipas and Nuevo Leon." These allies, together with Grant and Johnson's men and Fannin's men, "will prove amply sufficient" not just for victory, but will "place Texas in a situation to dictate to the neighboring states."[22] On paper at least, the Texan-federalist alliance was formidable. General Fernández had some 800 troops, Colonel González and Captain Canales led 350; Grant and Johnson commanded some 260 men; Fannin had 200-plus volunteers, including the Georgia Battalion; Plácido Benavides had as many as 47 mounted Tejano rancheros from Victoria scouting the Rio Grande in advance of Doctor Grant; and there were supposed to be at least 200 men recruited as "soldiers of fortune" who were sailing from New York on the brig *Mattawamkeag* and due to land "any day." (Alas, they would never arrive, being detained by the British at Nassau, Bahamas, under the charge of piracy, nor would another 100 regulars under Capt. Amasa Turner, whose schooner, ironically named the *Tamaulipas*, grounded on a bar at the mouth of the Brazos River.) The common assumption in Texas was that Santa Anna's armies, as John J. Linn recorded, "could not possibly arrive sooner than April 1."[23] There was also a widespread belief that enemy Mexicans were no match for resolute Anglo Texans and their American volunteers. Given Johnson's estimates, his assertion that Matamoros was "almost entirely without a garrison" and reports of "disaffection" in Santa Anna's ranks, the Matamoros expedition could hardly fail.

Moreover, Johnson's letter of February 2 also informed Fannin of an encouraging victory. Grant and his men had surprised and captured the pesky centralist force under Capt. Nicolás Rodríguez, which had regarrisoned Fort Lipantitlán and were now out on maneuvers south of San Patricio. They had captured a large *caballada* of horses, which Reuben B. Brown recounted was "to be recruited for the service of Urrea's division of the invading army." Grant's men suffered no losses in the fight. In Johnson's assessment, Grant's victory "leaves the road clear from Nueces to Rio Grande." In light of Johnson's seeming reliable intelligence and encouraging news, Fannin told Robinson in his same letter of February 4, "Matamoros is poorly supplied with troops—our friends are in power—I have reason to believe that, if a quick movement is made, not a shot will be fired." Fannin then declared his plans: "I shall proceed west and must beg of you to order the naval force to cooperate with me before Matamoros, between the 20 and 28. It is useless to urge the necessity, it is too apparent to require a second word."[24] Apparent or not, the four schooners of the fledgling Texas Navy, which the provisional government purchased and outfitted only in January, did Fannin little good, for only a few days later—in the face of the startling news that Urrea's army not only was advancing from Matamoros but even had defeated Grant and probably Johnson—he was forced to abandon the Matamoros expedition altogether.

7.

TRIUMPHANT MATAMOROS: THE MEXICAN EXPEDITION

BEFORE FANNIN ABANDONED the Matamoros expedition, Antonio López de Santa Anna already had ordered his own expedition to Matamoros under the command of Gen. José de Urrea. By January 15, Urrea set out for the river city and thence to begin the campaign into Texas to secure the coast and squash the approaching attackers. By month's end, the general would effectively occupy Matamoros, placate the agitated citizens of the Villas del Norte, recruit *soldados*, neutralize armed federalist rebels, and secure the vital support of other federalist forces as allies, including crucial rancheros in Texas. In the end, he would amass an army large enough to make Fannin's recruiting efforts and Johnson and Grant's volunteers altogether insufficient to attack Matamoros successfully, let alone occupy the city. Ultimately, Urrea would defeat the rebel forces in Texas at every encounter and would occupy the coastal prairie of Texas from San Patricio all the way to Brazoria—an achievement unrivaled by anyone else in the Mexican army.[1]

Santa Anna was well aware of U.S. intent to aid Texas rebels and of the federalists' "general plan of revolutionizing all over Mexico," as George Fisher had phrased his appeal to the Texas General Council when he urged it to authorize an expedition to Matamoros. Both Johnson and Fannin had emphasized that Lieutenant Governor Robinson keep silent on the question of independence for Texas until Mexican federalists had risen against the centralists, a maneuver which could readily be construed as duplicitous and manipulative toward their intended federalist allies.[2] Nevertheless, both Johnson and Fannin relied far too greatly and dangerously on promised federalist support, especially considering that such cooperation depended on Texas colonists remaining loyal to the Constitution of 1824 and that Mexican federalist commanders awaited Texas forces to make the initial move, essentially to prove their loyalty. This was grossly complicated because adventurers, mercenaries, and filibusters (rather than colonists) from the United States increasingly made up the bulk of Texas forces. But these volunteers professed no loyalty to Mexico or federalism and, amid a variety of personal motivations, sought the ultimate goal of "liberating" Texas for annexation to the United States.

Moreover, Grant, Johnson, and Fannin, who were leading these volunteers in an expedition to attack Matamoros, fatally underestimated the ability of Santa Anna's talented brigadier general, José de Urrea, whom historian Edwin R. Sweeney calls "an officer of exceptional intelligence, undaunted courage, [and] unquestioned integrity."[3] In the Texas Revolution story, Urrea is second only to Santa Anna as the most well-known Mexican general, but ironically he is perhaps the least fully appreciated. In most histories written in the United States in the nineteenth and twentieth centuries, Urrea was predictably condemned, as exemplified in David G. Burnet's public proclamation in 1836 branding Urrea as "the cold blooded murderer of the gallant Fannin and his noble band." Mexican histories, by contrast, offered praise, as when the state government of Sonora proclaimed in 1838 that their beloved federalist government "has been [made] possible by the patriotic efforts of our illustrious son, General José Urrea."[4] Likewise, in 1837 Mexican secretary of war José María Tornel praised "the brave General José Urrea," who "fulfilled the high hopes placed in his well-known courage and activity" through his "uninterrupted victories," which "well deserve the gratitude of [his] country." Despite his infamous association with the Goliad Massacre, Urrea's reputation has risen dramatically over the decades; recent historians praise him as talented, keen, capable, aggressive, skilled, energetic—one of Mexico's most able generals. Santa Anna himself praised Urrea's "well-earned reputation . . . in the Texas campaign" as "brilliant and fortune crowned in all his efforts."[5] Nevertheless, most of Urrea's long and distinguished, if controversial, career and his illustrious family heritage remain unfamiliar; even his name is given inaccurately or foreshortened in most English-language histories.

Born in 1797 into a distinguished Basque family in Tucson, Sonora (now Arizona), José Cosme de Urrea y Elías González was the great-grandson of pioneer rancher Bernardo de Urrea, who served as deputy *justicia mayor* (chief justice) to founder and explorer Juan Bautista de Anza. Bernardo de Urrea named his ranching headquarters *"artiz ona,"* a Basque phrase meaning "good oak"—a possible origin of Arizona's name. In the years to come, several men of the Urrea family would be stationed at the royal presidio in Tucson, including Mariano de Urrea and his wife, Gertrudis Elías González; the couple's firstborn son, José Cosme, was baptized at the presidio chapel on September 30, 1797. Both the Urrea and Elías families achieved distinguished military and civic careers. José Cosme de Urrea rapidly rose in the ranks from presidial cadet to a captain during the war for Mexican independence. As a staunch federalist, Urrea then fought in Tampico with Santa Anna against Isidro Barradas in 1829. He had convinced forces in Durango to support Santa Anna's rise to power in 1832 and established himself as a renowned Indian fighter against the Comanches there in 1835. Santa Anna promoted him to a general of brigade to lead the army moving into Texas to put down the Anglo American independence movement. Mexico City's official *Diario del Gobierno* praised Urrea's actions in Texas as distinguished by "honor, courage and civility"—which included, as Mexican historian Gerardo Palomo González discovered, using his personal credit to pay his troops. After his victorious service in Texas he would serve as commandant general and governor of Sonora as well as commandant general of Tamaulipas and Durango. Urrea would also participate in federalist uprisings in Sonora and Durango, for which he suffered defeat, capture, and temporary imprisonment. Nevertheless, he would fight with distinction against the invading U.S. army in the 1846–48 war with the United States, but would die August 1, 1849, during a cholera epidemic. As historian Henry F. Dobyns summarized his life, "Tucson native son José de Urrea y Elías González pursued a colorful, active career of political rebellions, defections, and disobedience to orders of the central government for forty years, with occasional flashes of progressive governance, supported always by strong partisans and opposed by bitter enemies." He was "noble and idealistic," as biographer Patricia Roche Herring described him, a man whose service for Mexico and Sonora ultimately "left behind an illustrious and honorable legacy."[6]

In 1836, Urrea set out toward Matamoros as Santa Anna ordered, commanding his independent division to defeat the oncoming Anglo American attackers. His force initially comprised only cavalry units—Robert C. Morris described them as "choice troops from the interior . . . armed, every one, with lance musket, pistols and sword." But his infantry, which was ordered to join him at Matamoros, were newly conscripted Mayan Indians in the Yucatán Activo Battalion from Tampico—barely trained, poorly equipped, and as events proved, ill-suited to face the northers of the Texas winter.[7]

As a necessary first measure, the general sought to squelch any potential federalist cooperation with the rebels in Texas. Despite a violent, rainy norther, he traveled throughout the Villas del Norte, recording that among these citizens he found a "great adherence to the constitution of 1824" and anxiety about the centralizing efforts of Santa Anna, but also that they believed the colonists in Texas were still upholding loyalty to federalism as well. In Urrea's judgment, this made the norteños "disposed to take up arms and join their [the Texans'] cause." Shrewdly understanding the circumstances, the general reassured and placated agitated norteños, appealed to their patriotism, and effectively persuaded his countrymen that the Texans, despite their federalist rhetoric, were disloyal and duplicitous—traitors, in fact, angling for independence. As Lt. Col. Enrique de la Peña remembered, "This commander omitted no means to convince the inhabitants of those townships of the bad faith with which the Texans were acting." As General Urrea himself recorded, "I took advantage of every opportunity to make them [norteños] keep the peace, disclosing to them the true views of the [Texas] colonists, thus succeeding in keeping them quiet."[8] He took measures to neutralize those actively engaged in aiding the Texas cause, like those of "ex-colonel" José María González, capturing many, but then, after reproving them, he incorporated them under his own personal command. De la Peña recounted that they "rendered very useful services afterward." Moreover, Urrea worked to secure the support of "loyal" federalists, such as Gen. Francisco Vital Fernández, who furnished Urrea's army with needed supplies. General Fernández, it will be remembered, had been charged by Tamaulipas governor José Antonio Fernández's decree of December 8 to raise a large volunteer force to defend the fatherland from the attacks of Texas rebels and "teach [them] a lesson"—a lesson Urrea was now empowered to teach. On January 31, Urrea arrived in Matamoros, where he utilized the city's fortifications, awaited his assigned infantry, recruited troops, and prepared for his campaign northward to secure coastal Texas. The strategic river city was at long last occupied through a successful Matamoros expedition—albeit from the Mexican side.[9]

On February 16, Urrea sent a scouting party under Fort Lipantitlán commander Nicolás Rodríguez to explore the road to the Nueces. Temporarily leaving about 200 men at Matamoros, Urrea crossed the Río Bravo the next day (he recorded that it took ten hours to do so) with approximately 188 cavalry followed by 205 infantry, baggage, and trains. Significantly, Urrea sought to ally Tejanos to his cause, just as he had other norteños. Despite their devotion to Texas and ardent federalism, Urrea persuaded many, probably most, Tejano rancheros in the area of San Patricio, Refugio, Goliad, and even Victoria of the disloyalty of the Anglo American rebels. These men—perhaps as many as 200, notably Carlos and Vicente de la Garza, Juan Letona, José María and Pedro Valdez, Juan and Agustín Moya, Encarnación Vásquez, Guadalupe de los Santos, and Salvador and Jesús "Comanche" Cuéllar—were increasingly incensed, as Mexicans, at their disdainful treatment by Anglo Americans. "They subsequently rendered very good service during the campaign as guides and scouts," Urrea wrote. In fact, they were vital in defeating Texan designs on Matamoros. As Creed Taylor put it, "Spies and emissaries informed him [Urrea] of the raid into the Rio Grande Valley and the position and the numbers of the Texans at San Patricio."[10] By contrast, the federalist Tejanos of Victoria, such as Plácido Benavides, José María Carbajal, and Fernando De León, who continued to support the revolution, were in the minority.

Urrea's actions to gain norteño and Tejano support, unknown to Johnson and Fannin, effectively nullified Johnson's optimistic appraisal of February 2. Moreover, Fannin's faith in Johnson's unrealistically positive view was shattered on February 7 from alarming intelligence gathered by Plácido Benavides, who had been in touch with the alcalde of Matamoros and Colonel González upriver at Camargo. "The inhabitants of Tamaulipas are generally in favor of [the Constitution of 1824]," Benavides reported, "but are so much oppressed by the military, many of the principal men having been arrested they are completely fettered." Moreover, "the people of Tamaulipas as well as those of the Rio Grande complain much of Dimitt's proclamation [of independence], and would have acted with more decision were it not for that act, but they fear it is now almost impossible." He confirmed that González's cavalry force was indeed "entirely dispersed," with twenty-two men taken prisoner (they were actually now in service under Urrea's personal command), and that the army at Matamoros under Urrea now numbered a thousand men or more, including lancer cavalry. Benavides dispelled a rumor that Santa Anna himself was already with the army at Matamoros, but "ascertained beyond all doubt" that El Presidente was indeed moving to invade Texas and suppress the rebellion through separate campaigns aimed at Goliad and San Antonio "simultaneously." Further, Santa Anna reportedly was using Matamoros as a trap to defeat the Texan expedition of which he had knowledge, for he planned to "draw the Troops of Texas out" in order to "throw a strong force in their rear while he makes his attack on the upper part of the Colonies." Always alluring, the pearl on the Río Bravo was now effectively the bait. Therefore, Benavides advised avoiding the city altogether, stressing instead that most Texan forces should concentrate troops at Béxar even as others were "retained in this area." Benavides's warning was enclosed in a communication to Fannin from Major Morris at San Patricio, to whom Benavides gave the information before leaving again to rejoin his company of rancheros with Grant's men.[11]

Before Benavides left Camargo, he sent Blas Herrera with a message to Béxar warning that "I have received a very certain notice, that the commander in chief, Antonio López de Santa Anna, marches for the city of San Antonio to take possession thereof" with a sizable army of ten thousand infantry and three thousand cavalry. (Herrera arrived at Béxar at 1:00 a.m. on February 11, and delivered his urgent missive to Antonio Manchaca during a festive ball being given in David Crockett's honor. Bowie, fluent in Spanish, urgently directed the warning to Travis, who reckoned it would take Santa Anna thirteen or fourteen days to reach Béxar.) Benavides left Camargo probably February 6 to join Grant at San Patricio. In the meantime, Grant and Johnson, leading "forty-five picked men," according to Creed Taylor—who also noted Johnson was "accompanying the expedition as second in command"—had been capturing much-needed horses in the expanse between the Nueces and Rio Grande in order to secure mounts for the Matamoros expedition. Of course, many of these animals roamed on private ranchos. As Taylor recounted, "In the valley of the Rio Grande on the Texas side roamed vast caballadas of horses, the property of Mexican citizens in Matamoros." The party crossed the Arroyo Colorado and "approached within eight or ten miles of Matamoros." Using "the tactics of the Comanches"—stealth, quickness, thievery—they "soon secured all the horses they wanted." By the time Grant returned to San Patricio, however, the party had only about 100 horses, "having lost a large number along the route." In part this was because "a furious 'norther' accompanied by rain and sleet beat down upon them, and during the night two of the men and a number of the horses died from the effects of the extreme cold."[12] General Urrea's army would encounter this same adversary of nature with similar results—but he would also use it to his advantage.

Benavides's disturbing warning did cause Fannin to abandon the Matamoros project—but now what was he to do? Adding to the confusion was a letter Fannin received from Johnson, dated February 9 from San Patricio, which claimed startling information in light of Benavides's intelligence. Reflecting Grant's influence, Johnson pleaded that Fannin "should be aware of the actual state of Matamoros more clearly than I can state in a public letter to avoid mens names being bandied about while they are still in the power of the enemy." Apparently Grant had reestablished contact with General Fernández and Don Pedro Lemus, the commandant general and inspector of the Eastern Interior Provinces. (Stephen F. Austin had assessed Lemus as "a man of high honor & liberal principles and a Gentleman.") Lemus met with Santa Anna in Saltillo and, in Johnson's words, was still trustworthy for "acquiring essential information & not incurring suspicion."[13] In Johnson's ever-optimistic assessment, "If a force from 3 [to] 400 men is sent agst Matamoros [meaning Grant, Johnson, and Fannin's combined force], Vital Fernández, who commands with 800 Taumalipas troops, will immediately join you—And the whole of the frontier towns will immediately follow . . . Time is precious & not a moment should be lost." With Matamoros under attack, Santa Anna would be compelled to respond, thus relieving "Bexar or Goliad or any point of Texas" of immediate danger. "The true policy is to unite all your forces here, leaving a small force in Bexar & Goliad & proceed without delay into the interior." Johnson appeared dauntless. "I can raise the whole country agst him [Santa Anna] & then the interior must move so as to compel him to a retrograde movement. . . . Quickness in your present movements will prove the salvation of Texas . . . All depends upon you." Johnson's letter included additional intelligence (in error) "from a person of credit in Saltillo" that "very serious movements" were underway in Zacatecas and Guadalajara, which would cause Santa Anna "to return incognito to the interior." This would leave General Filisola in charge of the army, which Johnson saw as "equal to a victory to us as Felisola is an old woman." Then, leaving Robert C. Morris in charge of a small contingent at San Patricio, Johnson and Grant again set out southward to meet up with Benavides, Fernández, González, Canales, and their presumed federalist allies.[14]

Filisola notwithstanding, not only did Johnson and Grant fatally underestimate General Urrea, but their intelligence sources regarding Gen. Vital Fernández and General Lemus made no mention of Tamaulipas governor José Antonio Fernández's decree of December 8, calling federalists to volunteer under General Fernández to defeat the "*indignos colonos*" of Texas—who now included substantial numbers of filibusters and mercenaries from the United States. Moreover, Lemus had met with Santa Anna at Saltillo to argue that El Presidente's invasion of Texas should proceed from Monterrey rather than Monclova in order to defeat the rebel attackers rumored to be heading to Matamoros. Perhaps the rumor that Benavides reported was true after all, that federalists and centralists temporarily united as patriotic Mexicans and were indeed using Matamoros as the fruit of temptation to draw these deceitful attackers and filibusters to their doom. At any rate, in light of Benavides's warning, Fannin, acting decisively and quickly, sent reinforcements under William G. Cooke to aid Morris at San Patricio and retrieve the artillery, and removed his headquarters from Refugio to Goliad. La Bahía, he argued, was more defensible and "advantageously located for a depot of reinforcements, clothing, provisions and military stores," which he anticipated would be coming via ports on Aransas and Matagorda Bays.[15]

Compounding the situation, the General Council (or more accurately, its "Advisory Committee," since it was without quorum) and Lieutenant Governor Robinson, in whom Fannin had chosen to place his allegiance, began sending dangerously mixed messages. Owing to Benavides's ominous warning, Robinson ordered Fannin to fortify and defend Goliad and even Béxar and to use great caution in battling the enemy until reinforced, since "a defeat of your command would prove our ruin." He gave Fannin significant discretion by countermanding "all former orders given by my predecessor, Genl. Houston or myself," and advised him instead to "obey any orders you deem Expedient." Incredibly, in several communications, both the council and lieutenant governor still pressed the ever more disconcerted Fannin as late as February 15 to proceed "to the accomplishment of the expedition" toward the Rio Grande as planned. Robinson, stressing that Béxar and Goliad would not be readily attacked—an astonishing assertion, given the circulating reports—wrote to Fannin on February 13, that the enemy "will endeavour to throw reinforcements into Matamoras is more than probable—Therefore you will always Keep in view the original objects of the campaign against [Matamoros], and dash upon it, as soon as it is prudent to do so in your opinion." Robinson also indicated he was going to order one-third of the "Militia" to Fannin's command. On February 15, the advisory committee of the General Council advised Fannin that no retrograde movement was necessary for him "or any of the troops designed for Matamoros" because new militia units "independent of the forces first designed for the Matamoras expedition" would prove "amply sufficient" in the defense of Béxar and Goliad against any centralist force crossing the Rio Grande. This remarkable report surely mystified Fannin, given the complete lack of response of the colonists to his own calls for help. Emphasizing that "every effort should be made, to sustain the expedition to Matamoros," the advisory committee ordered Fannin to maintain Copano and San Patricio and to proceed forthwith.[16] Alas, the promised militia help never materialized—just as Fannin had feared.

In Fannin's defense, it must be said that however strategic or realistic the capture of Matamoros may once have been, in light of new information that warned of the looming advance of the Mexican armies under Santa Anna and Urrea, these orders appear to be reckless, self-seeking, even dishonest. Indeed, in the face of Houston's jockeying for power and Smith's actions, the justification of the political conduct of the council and lieutenant governor toward Smith and Houston depended upon the success of the Matamoros campaign. The orders to "dash upon [Matamoros] as soon as it is prudent to do so" and a companion order Robinson issued to "not to make a retrograde movement, but to wait orders and reinforcements"[17] would haunt and immobilize Fannin, and in part, lead to the defeat of his army and to Houston's charge that the Matamoros expedition was the root of all evil. On the other hand, General Urrea's successful patriotic strategy of uniting Tamaulipan federalists, matamorenses, and Tejanos with his army against the Texas rebels appears in stark contrast to the fateful division, dispute, consternation and lack of leadership in the Texas ranks.

On February 9 or 10, Grant proceeded south once more (and fatefully for the last time) from San Patricio toward Matamoros, leading about fifty-three men—twenty-six volunteers from the United States in addition to Benavides's mounted company, now numbering perhaps twenty-seven rancheros. From San Patricio, Cooke soon reported to Fannin with heartening news from Grant and Morris delivered by "a Mexican officer in full uniform," likely Lt. Jesús "Comanche" Cuéllar, a double agent that Paul D. Lack says "had turned coats so often as to earn the suspicion of both sides." Still, Col. Francisco Garay, in Urrea's command, recorded in his diary (quoted by General Filisola) that despite the questionable activities of Cuéllar, "both he and his brother always carried out with honor [*siempre honradamente*] what they were told to do, and their zeal and unselfishness with which they served in the campaign were constant."[18]

Based on Cuéllar's information, Cooke reported that Morris—and accordingly Benavides—apparently "had been misinformed." General Fernández was indeed willing to unite with the Texans at the Rio Grande with 1,800 men! Confounding things further, Morris even informed Fannin (according to Cooke) that he "no longer intended to serve the Govt. of Texas" because he "had received the appointment to the command of a Regiment in the Federal service of Mexico."[19] In addition, as San Patricio founder John McMullen remembered, Grant had received intelligence that Capt. Antonio Canales Rosillo was at Camargo upriver from Matamoros with 200 federalists, "and by going to that place the[y] would get all the people of the towns on the Rio Grande to Join them." The news regarding Fernández and Canales galvanized Morris, Grant, Johnson, and Benavides into departing San Patricio with their men to head again for the Rio Grande, confident of—in fact, desperate for—federalist aid. Yet, when Urrea occupied Matamoros, he had already drawn upon General Fernández and his "Volunteers of the Fatherland" (as Gov. José Antonio Fernández called them) for needed supplies and on the "generous hospitality" of the city. Further, Urrea had secured the patriotism of the norteños, including the residents of Camargo, where Canales found it best to realign himself. Thus, however much Grant's information regarding federalist help had once been accurate, Urrea's actions nullified it, rendering Benavides's earlier warning as closer to the truth. Grant, Johnson, Morris, and Benavides would be on their own.[20]

Upon receiving Cooke's letter, Fannin, then still at Refugio, had to have been exasperated. He dispatched Burr H. Duval's company on February 11 with teams to retrieve the artillery Johnson and Grant left behind at San Patricio. Fannin then withdrew to Goliad on February 12, leaving a company under Amon B. King at Refugio to help evacuate colonists stranded there. That Fannin appreciated his circumstances more than did Johnson and Grant is indicated in a letter to Lieutenant Governor Robinson of February 16—by which time Urrea, unbeknownst to Fannin, was already scouting ahead as far as the Nueces River. In this letter, Fannin noted that young J. Hampton Kuykendall and a Mexican companion had just arrived from Matamoros with news that the Santa Anna's army was crossing into Texas in three divisions, one to take Béxar, another aimed at Goliad, and the third under Santa Anna himself. Fannin indicated that he was taking measures to withdraw to San Antonio and he emphasized that evidence now convinced him that the Texans must rely only on themselves, that federalist help was not forthcoming as hoped. "No aid need be expected from Mexicans," he wrote.[21] Benavides had been right.

Consequently, the dominoes of the Texan Matamoros expedition began to fall. Tragically, accompanying Fannin's growing awareness of the seriousness of the situation, he began doubting his leadership abilities. Therefore, he pressed the council to relieve him of the burden of command—which is ironic, given that his personal ambitions, previous experience, and limited West Point training helped him obtain the very position from which he now sought relief. Fannin's somber epistles from February 7 to March 1, 1836, reveal a husband and father longing for his wife and children, a patriot angry at the colonists of Texas—"the sluggards"—who were not responding to his repeated calls to arms or even bringing provisions, and a soldier feeling abandoned by the government he trusted yet still hoping for the promised reinforcements. Fannin knew full well the possible consequences he faced. "I have orders from you *not* to make a *retrograde movement*, but to await orders and reinforcements," he wrote Lieutenant Governor Robinson, apparently disregarding the leeway that Robinson had earlier given him, to "obey any orders you deem Expedient." But Fannin stressed his desire to "have leave to bring off my *brave foreign volunteers*, in the best manner I may be able. If we should fail in the effort, and fall a sacrifice to the criminal indifference, cold and unpardonable apathy and neglect . . . peradventure, drop a tear over our memory." In spite of it all, he managed to sign himself as "Hoping for the best, being prepared for the worst, I am in a devil of a bad humor."[22]

Meanwhile, Johnson, Grant, and Benavides's men had arrived at the Santa Rosa ranch, about thirty miles from Matamoros, when their horses gave out in the unforgiving thorn scrub. Grant received his last warning, "through the interfarence of his friends" (according to an account by San Patricio empresarios John McMullen or James McGloin), that if they continued, they would not return: "It was only a plan of the enemy to get them [there and] to destroy them." Johnson and thirty-four men returned to San Patricio with more than one hundred animals, which Grant had purchased from area rancheros with cash or promissory certificates. But

Grant proceeded toward Camargo with Morris and twenty-some volunteers from the United States plus Benavides and his twenty-some rancheros. Neither Johnson nor Grant was apparently aware that Urrea's advance forces had pressed into the vicinity; they wrongly assumed Urrea was still in Matamoros and that Camargo was safe. By contrast, the astute Mexican general was kept informed (he described the intelligence as "exact information") of Johnson and Grant's movements through numerous scouts and spies, which included Don Salvador Cuéllar (brother of Jesús "Comanche") and other disaffected Tejano rancheros—likely including the very ones from whom Grant had earlier purchased horses.[23]

In spite of a particularly harsh norther, which Urrea described as "very raw and excessively cold" with continuous rain—his dragoons "so numbed by the cold that they could hardly speak"—the Mexican general cautiously surrounded the village of San Patricio. Taking advantage of the inclement weather, he surprised Johnson's men occupying various houses at about three thirty in the morning on February 27 and defeated them in the battle of San Patricio. Local tradition tells that Urrea, in working an almost Mosaic "passover," had contacted loyalists in the village and requested them to place lit candles in their windows, thereby marking the dark houses as the targets for attack. Utilizing other intelligence, Urrea ordered a separate foray to the nearby ranch of Don Julián de la Garza, where Capt. Rafael Pretalia similarly surprised and defeated a detachment of Johnson's men guarding the precious caballada of horses. In this double debacle, Johnson was among those few who escaped; the escapees eventually made their way to Refugio, where an urgent dispatch was sent to Goliad. Fannin learned of Johnson's fate on February 28. Urrea sent the remaining survivors to Matamoros to be imprisoned.[24]

Ordering his dragoons to replace tired horses with fresh mounts, Urrea then backtracked to find Grant's men, who may have made it to the ranches at Camargo and purchased more horses, but in the process learned that their federalist contacts were no longer helpful and even proved deceitful. Grant and his men (forty to fifty "picked riflemen" as Urrea's intelligence estimated them) left the Rio Grande on February 27, heading back to San Patricio. Indeed, while traditional histories give Grant's number to be only twenty-six volunteers from the United States, this ignores Benavides's rancheros, who likely accounted for another twenty-seven. Urrea's intelligence was close to the truth after all. Urrea pursued with eighty lancer dragoons, a contingent of Yucatán infantry, a few soldados from Fort Lipantitlán under Nicolás Rodríguez, and even mounted Tejano rancheros and reportedly Karankawa Indians from the Goliad-Victoria area under Carlos de la Garza. On March 2—the same day the Texas Convention declared independence—the Mexican general

The dreaded Mexican lancers were crucial in Gen. José de Urrea's defeat of Dr. James Grant's Matamoros expedition at the battle of Agua Dulce Creek and James Fannin's men at the battles of Refugio and the Coleto. John Frost, *History of Mexico and Its Wars* (1882), 193. From author's collection.

Mexican Lancer.

ambushed and defeated Grant's command in the battle of Agua Dulce Creek. The location was near El Lugar del Banquete, site of the annual fiestas celebrating the close ties between the people of San Patricio and Matamoros. In a communication to Col. José M. Guerra, Rodríguez confirmed that Urrea used his lancers to great effect. Urrea reported killing forty-two, which likely included all the rancheros save Benavides, and capturing three others, who were sent to Matamoros. Only about five escaped, though there may have been several more. As historian Stephen Hardin emphasizes, "More Tejanos—perhaps as many as twenty-four—died at Agua Dulce than in any other battle of the Texas Revolution."[25]

Grant, recognized by his pursuers, was killed brutally in the fray. According to Reuben R. Brown, an eyewitness who was wounded, captured, and imprisoned at Matamoros but later escaped (and left conflicting accounts), the unfortunate Grant, after outriding the pursuing dragoons by some seven miles or more, was eventually pierced by one, perhaps more, lances. With his horse failing, he dismounted or fell off the saddle and may have been trying to surrender, but was then run through with swords by several Mexican officers. Brown asserted that Grant "was well known to them . . . and they had a bitter grudge against him," claiming even that a substantial reward was offered "for his head." Urrea's diary mentions none of this, but Lieutenant Colonel de la Peña recorded that Urrea regretted that the "well known and prominent" Grant had not been captured alive, for he would have been a valuable prize. Grant was well known for his wealth, estates, and politics as an outspoken federalist and former deputy president of the state legislature. But now he was known for leading a group of armed filibusters and mercenaries to attack Matamoros, supposedly in the name of Mexican federalism. Despite Urrea's direction that "every effort [be] exerted to make him a prisoner," some of his men got carried away, whether from patriotic zeal, revenge, or the rush of battle—something Houston also could not control at San Jacinto's bloodbath. De la Peña even suggested greed and thievery as motives: "The bait of his [Grant's] silver saddle, of his flashy firearms and other valuable jewels, provoked one of the 'cossack' officers to shamefully murder him." There is no reason to doubt de la Peña's observation that "eyewitnesses assert that Grant defended himself courageously, and on many occasions have we heard General Urrea lament his death."[26] But before this chilling finale, Grant had dispatched Benavides, who was still riding with him and Brown, to attempt an escape to warn Fannin of Urrea's proximity. The dauntless Benavides, who Brown said was "better mounted than Grant or myself," outrode the dragoons and successfully delivered the devastating message to Fannin at Goliad. He then returned to his rancho at Victoria to prepare for Urrea's now inevitable advance, which did not bode well for the residents of his town, who had thrown their loyalty, wealth and resources to the Texas cause.[27]

Owing to the spirited leadership of General Urrea—whose own Matamoros campaign was overwhelmingly successful—it is terribly ironic that the only members of Grant and Johnson's Matamoros expedition to reach their destination were those captured and imprisoned survivors of the battles of San Patricio and Agua Dulce Creek. The fiasco awaiting Fannin's men would only add to this dramatic irony. Many years later, Johnson would write his own version of history, in particular to address Houston's severe condemnations and scapegoating that the Matamoros expedition was, as Houston put it, "the prime cause of all the disasters that befell the country." Eventually published as *A History of Texas and Texans*, Johnson sought to exonerate himself and defend the character and patriotism of Grant and Fannin, who in death could not defend themselves. As for Houston's role, Johnson was clear: "So far as the failure of the expedition against Matamoras, and the disasters that befell the Texan army subsequently, no man contributed more to that end than did General Houston."[28] The acrimonious blame, in effect, was mutual. Although Houston's assessment is arguably more accurate, both fail, understandably, to acknowledge the decisive skill of their adversary, José de Urrea. The Texan strategy to capture Matamoros, however credible it once may have been, proved paramount in paralyzing the Texas provisional government and in the defeat of Texas forces, indirectly at the Alamo and directly at San Patricio, Agua Dulce Creek, Refugio, and Goliad. Moreover, these disas-

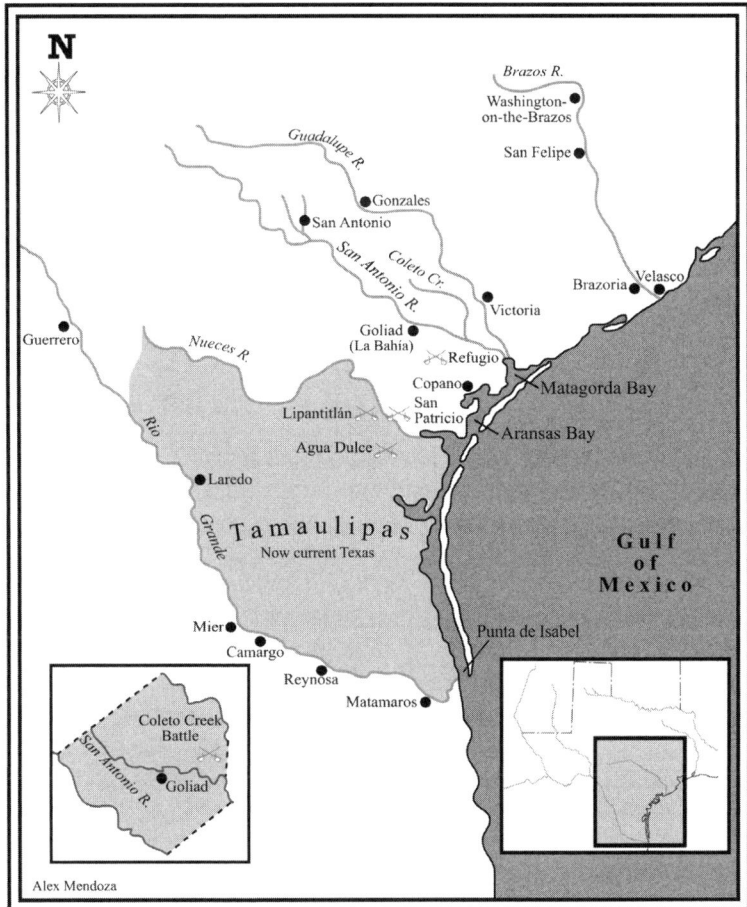

Significant sites related to the Matamoros expeditions. Places of battle are marked with crossed swords.

ters, which both Houston and Johnson decried, were in effect triumphs of the Mexican and loyalist Tejano forces under General Urrea. His expedition to occupy Matamoros and benefit from the city's resources and its federalist allies (as Texas strategists had hoped to do) was indeed pivotal in the revolution for him and his victorious Mexican army, which remained undefeated and would occupy the Texas coastal plain from San Patricio to Brazoria. "So great was the reputation he had established during the campaign," wrote Lieutenant Colonel de la Peña about Urrea, "he was looked upon as an anchor of salvation."[29] Simply put, Urrea succeeded.

Meanwhile, Fannin, having abandoned the Matamoros expedition and withdrawn to Goliad, engaged his men in repairing and fortifying the old La Bahía presidio, which he re-christened Fort Defiance. In the wake of Urrea's advance, he was still torn between standing siege at Goliad or reinforcing Travis at the Alamo.[30] Travis's pleas for help reached Goliad on February 25, but Fannin's poorly organized and dangerously undersupplied relief effort broke down on the banks of the San Antonio River only two miles from the fort, forcing them to return. This produced bitter resentment among his men, especially the San Antonio (New Orleans) Greys, causing many to lose confidence in him, which in turn depressed Fannin still further. In a letter to Lieutenant Governor Robinson, Fannin indicated not only that he knew Urrea was en route but also that the Mexican army already besieging Travis at the Alamo would next descend on Goliad. Therefore, he figured he had to fall back to his supplies, which were still on the coast southeast of Victoria at Matagorda, Dimmitt's Landing, and Cox's Point. Even though Urrea was hunting down Johnson and Grant at this time, he was kept informed of Fannin's actions. On February 27, the general "ordered two parties of twenty men each to reconnoiter the vicinity of Goliad" and "detailed, also, two men of the town to observe the enemy." Their reports assessed fairly accurately Fannin's troop strength and even artillery.[31]

From a strategic point of view, given Fannin's critical shortage of supplies, limited manpower, and knowledge that Santa Anna's large army was already at San Antonio and Urrea's force was forthcoming, the Goliad commander's decision to abandon the effort to relieve Travis was valid, despite the criticism the decision has historically suffered. Since Goliad was recognized as the gateway to, and the only remaining defendable position of, the coastal plain, Fannin's initial decision of standing siege at Fort Defiance seemed to make sense—though Goliad's strategic value was questionable if Travis and Bowie lost Béxar.[32] But this was only one of many difficulties at Fort Defiance—an appropriate name, as there were many things being confronted, resisted, and challenged there. Various letters indicate that these resolute volunteers were "nearly naked" in ragged clothing, most had shoes in disrepair, some even barefoot—all certainly exacerbated by the brutally cold and wet norther—plus there was no food other than fresh beef. Falling back to the supplies on the coast therefore had great merit, especially in light of the Alamo disaster. Sadly, letters also indicate that "much dissention prevails among the Volunteers" and that "Col. Fannin . . . is unpopular." Another wrote that the "majority of the soldiers don't like him" because "he wishes to become great without taking the proper steps to attain greatness." Such signs of increasing resentment among his men were compounded by Fannin's own inner demons and mounting depression. Further, Fannin remained mostly ignorant of General Urrea's movements other than the news of Johnson's defeat at San Patricio and Grant's at Agua Dulce. In light of these circumstances, Fannin's strategic sense told him to abandon Goliad and withdraw to Victoria and the coast toward the supplies; he also hoped to connect with reinforcements rumored to be on the way. Rather than pursue that option, however, he prepared Fort Defiance for assault, its long-eager defenders now increasingly anxious to engage an enemy whose proficiency they greatly underrated.[33]

Like a tragic Shakespearean figure, Fannin seemed paralyzed. Ordered by the General Council not to make a retrograde movement, he remained at Goliad awaiting instructions to the contrary. "I am resolved to await your orders, let the consequence be what it may." Like Travis, Fannin was ever frustrated that the colonists did not answer his call to arms. He decried in sober earnestness, "Why halt ye between two opinions," quoting the Prophet Elijah (1 Kings 18:21), who admonished the people to choose between following God or Baal—but the verse ends, fatefully in Fannin's case, "and the people answered him not a word."[34] Apparently neither Travis nor Fannin appreciated how much the Mexican army now inspired fear, how the question of independence divided the colonists, and especially how the actions of the American volunteers had alienated most Tejanos, who remained proud and patriotic Mexicans regardless of their concerns about Santa Anna. Fannin wrote prophetically to Robinson on February 22, "But I say to you, candidly, and without fear of Mexican arms, that unless the people of Texas, forthwith, turn out in mass . . . those *now* in the field will be sacrificed, and the battle that should be fought *here*, will be fought East of the Brassos, and probably the Trinity." Robinson's reply of March 6 (the day the Alamo fell) reflected a sad helplessness to aid Fannin, yet stubbornly defended the council's political position. Still, Robinson advised him to "use your own discretion to remain where you are or retreat as you may think best for the safety of the brave Volunteers Under your command." Washing his hands of the mess, Robinson indicated that a new government was being formed by the convention and advised Fannin to direct his future communications to them. Fannin's hopes were undoubtedly stirred by Robinson's information that "Captn. Dimitt with 200 men . . . [is] marching for your relief" and that Houston "has been ordered to the Army by the convention forthwith."[35]

Despite the lack of support, the commander of Fort Defiance seemed to remain resolute, devoted at least to a shadow of his original mission to take Matamoros. In a revealing letter to General Mexía on March 11, Fannin resolved that "circumstances unexpected and over which I had no control, have placed me, where I cannot retreat, but in disgrace. This

I am not disposed to suffer—rather preferring to encounter death in any shape." He continued by arguing "if I had men over whom I could exercise reasonable authority, I should glory in the present opportunity as I should most certainly do myself some credit, and the country great service; and teach Genl. Sa. Anna a lesson, which he might remember, and the states of Mexico profit by." Fannin correctly perceived that the new convention had or soon would declare independence, but, he told Mexía, this will "not interfere with your favourite project. You can go ahead . . . and may calculate upon aid from Texas—and her Volunteers," adding, "I hope I may aid in it."[36]

On March 4, the newly convened convention appointed Houston as commander-in-chief of all regular, volunteer, and militia troops. Now having the authority he had long sought, Houston attempted to take over Fannin's command. Arriving at Gonzales on March 11, he issued Fannin the long-awaited orders to retreat to Victoria and ultimately Gonzales, also enclosing the latest information that the Alamo had very likely fallen, with no survivors. But by the time Houston's order arrived, Fannin had already engaged Urrea. Through a series of poor, if compassionate, decisions and tragic events, the Goliad commander divided his main army. He sent Ward and the Georgia Battalion to Refugio to assist King, whom he had earlier ordered to evacuate stranded colonists there. But Ward would find that King had already begun battling Urrea's advance cavalry—most being invaluable mounted Tejano rancheros alienated from the Anglo American version of the Texas cause who had instead answered Urrea's call. Fannin then attempted to retreat to Victoria, as ordered, with the main army.[37]

Houston's dismal assessment of Fannin's situation proved tragically accurate. "I could not rely on any co-operation from him," he wrote to James Collinsworth of the convention's military committee on March 13. Houston also took this opportunity to cast history in his favor. "The projected expedition to Matamoras, under the *agency* of the council has already cost us over two hundred and thirty-seven lives; and where the effects are to end, none can foresee. . . . I fear La Bahia (Goliad) is in *siege*."[38] Indeed, within a week of this letter, Urrea would defeat King's, Ward's, and Fannin's separated commands piecemeal in the battle of Refugio and the battle of Coleto (Goliad). Urrea called the latter "la batalla de Encinal del Perdido," referring to the live oak grove of Perdido Creek; ironically, *perdido* means "lost." The survivors of these engagements, more than 400 men—including Fannin, with a crippling thigh wound, and Ward with the remnant of the Georgia Battalion that had escaped Refugio, only to be captured in the Guadalupe River bottom near the Victoria coast— would not be sent to Matamoros as prisoners but would be marched back to Presidio La Bahía instead. Santa Anna issued insistent orders to carry out the congressional decree of December 30, 1835, which commanded death to all armed foreign rebels. Despite Urrea's plea for leniency, most of these men (save a handful who were spared or escaped) were executed by firing squads under Col. José Nicolás de la Portilla on Palm Sunday, March 27, 1836—the infamous Goliad Massacre. Undefeated, though deeply disturbed by the massive executions, Gen. José Cosme de Urrea continued his victorious march, occupying Victoria and the coast toward Brazoria, causing in his wake a "runaway scrape" similar to that being caused by Santa Anna after capturing San Antonio.[39] Now the folly, as Houston saw the Matamoros campaign, was reaping the whirlwind.

Yet the whirlwind shifted its course. In April, amid the month-long Runaway Scrape, Houston was retreating east with the remnant of the Texas army, now consisting mostly of Texas colonists because the majority of volunteers from the United States had been killed under Grant, Johnson, Fannin, and Travis. Houston was purportedly to meet up with U.S. Maj. Gen. Edmund Pendleton Gaines and his army of American regulars, which the Andrew Jackson administration had ordered to the Sabine River to "defend" the border between Texas and Louisiana. Whatever plot for U.S. aid or even armed involvement might have been at play, Houston led his army to one of the great victories in military history on April 21 near Lynch's Ferry on the San Jacinto River below its confluence with Buffalo Bayou. Controversy still haunts the battle, but without question Santa Anna's segment of the Mexican army was thoroughly defeated; yet the remaining divisions, now including Urrea's, were poised to retaliate. However, the fortuitous capture at San Jacinto of His Excellency, El Presidente himself, made a Mexican counterattack unfeasible (out of concern for Santa Anna's life) and gave Houston the upper hand to negotiate a controversial treaty for the independence of Texas. In reality, as historian Will Fowler's superb biography makes clear, Santa Anna shrewdly committed himself to nothing more than a promising that a Texas commission could make its case for independence to the Mexican government (he insisted that, because he was a prisoner, anything he signed or said would hardly be ratified by Congress), and ordering the other divisions of the Mexican army under Generals Filisola, Ramírez y Sesma, and Urrea, to withdraw back to Matamoros. Even in this, Santa Anna's order purposefully transferred command of the army to Filisola and gave assertions to regroup.[40]

Mexican withdrawal and failure to counterattack was not due to orders, however, so much as to nature, as Gregg J. Dimmick shows in his book *Sea of Mud*. Punctuating a very wet spring that had already hindered the Mexican army with high waters, a brutal thunderstorm brought a nearly relentless deluge of rain the last week of April 1836, falling in torrents with cannonlike thunder, swelling rivers, and producing swamps that created a disaster for the Mexican army in what is now Wharton County, Texas. Slogging through knee-deep boggy mud, soldados began throwing away anything of weight—equipment, munitions, even muskets and provisions. There were no means to build fires, and dysentery also took a toll. In General Filisola's words, "*bestias, cañones, todo, podía decirse, nadaba en un mar de lodo*" ("beasts, cannons, everything could be said, swimming in a sea of mud"). "The cannon and the loaded pack mules sank in the mud when least expected," recorded José Enrique de la Peña. "In this tragic retreat fatigue was as great as privations were excessive. . . . Everything is misfortune, work, and hardship." Even the indefatigable Urrea, when his undefeated division rendezvoused with Filisola, was dumbfounded to discover the rest of the army not only in miserable retreat after San Jacinto, but suffering "in a mud hole where the men were hardly able to stand up." Shocked by the multitude of sick men, abandoned equipment and wagons, the otherwise indomitable Urrea wrote matter-of-factly that the "march was extremely painful," and the pervasive mud "threatened to engulf the men and the beasts." The Mexican army became utterly exhausted, disorganized and demoralized; accusations of blame abounded among the officers. "The major factor that had changed," Dimmick writes, "was not the number of troops, the strength of the Texans, or the Mexican leadership, but the fighting spirit and the equipment of the *soldados*, which had been decimated by nine days in the mud of the Mar de Lodo."[41] The storm turned the temporary setback of San Jacinto into a greater catastrophe that ended any immediate hope of a Mexican counterattack. There was nothing left to do but trudge back to Matamoros—the city of refuge and extravagant expectations, namesake of warrior priest and warrior saint—perhaps to try again.

8.
EPILOGUE: HERÓICA
MATAMOROS

"May Saint James destroy the enemy so that when we come again to Matamoros no hateful gringo *face will offend our eyes."*

—Don Santiago de Mendoza y Soría, character in *Caballero* by Jovita González and Eve Raleigh[1]

FROM THE MEXICAN POINT OF VIEW, regardless of Houston's victory at San Jacinto, the capture of Santa Anna, and the resulting Treaties of Velasco, Texas had been stolen by Anglos masquerading as colonists defending the Constitution of 1824 whose true intent was to annex Texas to the United States. In *Sea of Mud*, Gregg J. Dimmick exposes a number of issues that kept the demoralized Mexican army, having endured the *mar de lodo* and humiliating retreat back to Matamoros, from attempting a counterattack back into Texas, including accusations of blame between commanding generals Filisola and Urrea. In a frenzy of scapegoating, both generals published ultra-critical judgments of each other in 1838, resulting in a loss of focus, which in turn compounded a flurry of new confrontations in Mexico City between centralists and federalists in Santa Anna's absence. Even so, as Will Fowler asserts in his biography of Santa Anna, the captured president-general had "used all his powers of persuasion to come up with a treaty in which he did not commit himself to anything binding." Rather, the crafty fox "found a 'decorous' way out, which did not tie or bind the nation to recognizing the Texans' demands."[2]

Mexico did not recognize Texas independence, despite recognition of the new republic by the United States, England, and France. Rather, the centralist Mexican government launched several military expeditions from Matamoros into Texas in the 1840s to reassert rightful control against what historian Arturo Zárate-Ruiz calls "*los bandidos texanos*" (the Texan bandits). Centralists also tried to utilize Indian alliances to stir up dissension and strife in Texas. There is evidence that the infamous Great Comanche Raid of 1840, which terrorized the Guadalupe River valley with plundering, burning, killing settlers, and stealing horses, was part of a scheme, plotted in Matamoros, among centralists and Comanches to punish the citizens of Victoria along with its port of Linnville for aiding the federalist cause and supporting the Texas Revolution. Although Mexican forces in various operations temporarily occupied Refugio, Goliad, Victoria, and even San Antonio in 1842, these campaigns were unsuccessful. But then, Texan efforts to occupy areas south of the Nueces likewise failed.[3] Again Zárate-Ruiz apprises, "Only annexed to the United States could the Texans pursue their claim to extend the territorial boundaries to the Bravo."[4] Consequently, the controversial war with the United States in 1846–48 ended any notion that the land north of the Rio Grande was still part of Mexico and humiliated Mexico further when it lost the vast territory west of Texas all the way to California. This would set the tone between Mexico and the United States for the next half century. Manifest Destiny was seemingly insatiable.

Matamorenses paid a particularly high price for Texas independence and statehood; much like the Tejanos of South Texas, they were caught in the middle. The Matamoros economy was significantly hurt with the continued demands of the military, whose focus on the rebellion in Texas in turn caused increased Indian depredations and motivated robbers. Both Indians and robbers attacked the trade caravans, causing greatly curtailed trade. In April and August 1836 and again in March 1837, hundreds of Comanche warriors struck the ranches around Matamoros, with reports of one thousand Comanches within a league of Matamoros itself. Lipan Apache attacks also occurred in the vicinity. Because matamorenses had supplied the Mexican army's forays against the Texas rebels, town officials protested to the government that citizens were now greatly handicapped in carrying out their tasks of livelihood and defense. Bearing the brunt of Indian attack, Matamoros and other Villas del Norte appealed to the state legislature in 1841 to be exempted from the requirement of military service. Not only did the government deny the cities' petition but it also refused to offer aid in fighting the Indians, understandably greatly exacerbating existing tensions.[5]

Moreover, in the summer following the battle of San Jacinto, the fledgling Texas Navy even enforced a blockade of Matamoros in an effort to interfere with the Mexican army's plans to retake Texas. The blockade created harsh feelings toward the city's Anglo American merchants, causing most to leave; by November 1837, Americans owned only three commercial houses in Matamoros. This exodus in turn temporarily wreaked financial havoc—a measure of the city's dependence upon American trade and smuggled goods. Still, as Omar S. Valerio-Jiménez affirms, the "military commanders [in Matamoros] angrily accused residents of treason because 'forgetting the label of mexicanos, they continued trading with

the enemies of the nation, protecting them with clandestine commerce
. . . and in fact, recognizing the independence of Texas.'" But such accusations fell on deaf ears as matamorenses dealt with economic devastation;
these *fronterizos* continued in their long tradition of ignoring the orders
of the government that demanded much, but offered little benefit. As a
result, smuggling of goods greatly increased, especially foreign cottons, by
1838–39 when federalist insurrectionaries increased their control of the
area once again.[6]

Between 1838–40, unrepentant federalists in the northern Mexican states of Tamaulipas, Coahuila, and Nuevo León—again supported
by allies in Texas and New Orleans—attempted to create a Republic
of the Rio Grande, with its capital temporarily located at the Villa del
Norte town of Guerrero, Tamaulipas. Among the dignitaries were Jesús
de Cárdenas, president; the resilient Antonio Canales Rosillo (the "Chaparral Fox"), commander-in-chief of the army; and none other than José
María Jesús Carbajal—Plácido Benavides's brother-in-law and Stephen F.
Austin's godson—as secretary to the council. Revisionist Mexican historian Josefina Zoraida Vázquez asserts that the idea for the republic was in
reality only "born from letters sent to Texan newspapers as a true *wishful
thinking*" and called "La Repúblic Norte Mexicana."[7] Nonetheless, the
nascent revolution was defeated by Mariano Arista, commandant general
of Tamaulipas and general of the Mexican Army of the North. But General
Arista would not be victorious against Gen. Zachary Taylor's advancing
U.S. army. Not satisfied with the mere acquisition of Texas, "the degen-
erate sons of Washington," as Matamoros Gen. Francisco Mejía called
Taylor's soldiers, crossed the Nueces River with "perfidious conduct,"
invading Tamaulipas in early 1846.[8] It is worth noting that the invading
army used the same historic La Bahía Road traversed for more than a
century by Hispanic settlers, soldiers, travelers, and traders, only now it
was nicknamed "Taylor's Trail." General Taylor established Fort Texas (later
renamed Fort Brown) when his army reached the Rio Grande on March
26, 1846—one day short of the tenth anniversary of the unquestionably
perfidious Goliad Massacre.

Taylor's victories against Arista in the U.S.-Mexico war's initial battles
of Palo Alto and Resaca de la Palma on May 8 and 9, and the subsequent
American occupation of Matamoros—which, as Arturo Zárate-Ruiz
reminds us, resulted in matamorenses being "stripped of their local ter-
ritories"—were widely reported.[9] The name of the beleaguered river city
became better known throughout the United States than ever before. But
the city's name was misspelled more often than not in sources published in
the United States. "Matamoras" was the most common aberration, which
was the spelling adopted in the late 1840s by at least four river "border

towns" in Pennsylvania, Ohio, and Indiana to commemorate Taylor's victories. Denise Spellberg suggests that the seemingly innocent misspelling—the final "a" being feminine in Spanish rather than the masculine "o"—reveals not only a "sheer disdain for the indigenous language," but on a deeper level symbolizes the U.S. triumph over Mexico in its "implicit feminization of the enemy" and an "actual occupation of territory," literally inventing "a new space of occupation, a twisted, gendered linguistic trophy of conquest." This misspelling is also evidenced in the euphoria—which Robert W. Johannsen asserts "approached hysteria"—that quickly swept the United States following news of Taylor's victories as the public consumed rapidly produced plays, songs, books, and engraved pictures of the battles (including "The Bombardment of Matamoras," which never happened), wore Palo Alto hats, and drank Palo Alto root beer. Yet, Spellberg asserts that the town names "appear to unite separate, warring cultures symbolically," linking the Spanish conquest of Islam and then Mexico, the triumph of Mexico over imperial Spain, and of the United States over Mexico. "The naming of Matamoras reveals a history that defies easy dichotomies and challenges the notion of borderlands as fixed in time or place."[10] In the wake of the U.S. victories and occupation of Matamoros, the city again played its historic role as *la puerta*, the gateway, as Taylor's army then continued to stream into the interior of Mexico and on to victories at Monterrey, Saltillo, and Buena Vista, ultimately to occupy northern Mexico.

From the Mexican point of view, a more honorable renaming of Matamoros occurred as a result of yet another attempt by disquieted federalists in 1848–49 to foment rebellion in the northern Mexican states to create an independent federalist republic, this time called the Republic of the Sierra Madre. Again Matamoros was targeted as the pearl of great price. Carbajal again played a leading role, supplied by Brownsville pioneers Charles Stillman, Mifflin Kenedy, and Richard King. According to biographer Joseph E. Chance, Carbajal repeatedly recruited filibusters and mercenaries from both sides of the Rio Grande. Arturo Zárate-Ruiz reminds us that matamorenses distrusted Carbajal's connections with "many Texan filibusters in the pay of big traders—and smugglers [*los grandes comerciantes—y contrabadistas*]—of Brownsville." The city's actions under alcalde Macedonio Capistrán and Gen. Francisco Ávalos in helping to defeat Carbajal's *separatistas*—including resisting a ten-day siege, attacks, looting, and destruction of property—resulted in the state congress conferring upon the city the titles of "Unconquered" (*Invicta*) and "Heroic" (*Heróica*), and the national congress awarding the title of "Loyal" (*Leal*).[11] Hereafter, the river city would officially be known as "Heróica Matamoros."

The Brownsville & Matamoros (B&M) International Bridge, opened in 1910, was the first permanent bridge across the Rio Grande connecting Matamoros and Brownsville. Built as a swing-bridge to accommodate river traffic, it served pedestrians, animal-drawn traffic, automobiles and rail. Postcard based on a Robert Runyon photograph. From author's collection.

By 1858, H. Matamoros would enter a new golden age. Fetching lithographs of the city, with its cathedral dominating the skyline in an almost Edenic setting, appeared in respected news journals and books worldwide, such as *Harper's Weekly*, *Frank Leslie's Illustrated Newspaper*, the *Illustrated London News*, and *Le Journal illustré*, although often miscaptioned as "Matamoras." As the city served the premier cotton-growing region of Mexico, the government created a free trade zone (Zona Libre), which encouraged trade with the United States by making the border duty free—an effort also to counter Brownsville's emerging status as a smuggling center. During the American Civil War, in the wake of the Union Navy's blockade of Confederate ports, Matamoros thrived as the crucial overland destination for southern cotton via the same historic La Bahía Road (now dubbed the "Cotton Road") in the Confederacy's desperate strategy to ship cotton to Europe in exchange for supplies, medicines, and munitions. Surviving the French intervention (1862–67) and several devastating hurricanes, Matamoros rose again to become "one of the chief commercial ports of the world," as Warner P. Sutton, U.S. Consul-General in Matamoros, affirmed in 1888.[12] By the late nineteenth century and into the twentieth, economic and diplomatic ties would replace military matters— weathering several "boom-bust" cycles as well as the Mexican Revolution of 1910–20—as trade, cotton, industrialization, and eventually tourism

Charro Days Parade, Brownsville, Texas, 1938. The international Charro Days Fiesta, co-sponsored by the cities of Matamoros and Brownsville, has been celebrating a shared cultural heritage since 1937. Photograph. From author's collection.

literally bridged two cultures not so separated after all by a river called both Bravo and Grande. The growing relationship between Brownsville and Matamoros underscored this transformation as the two cities increasingly mirrored one another. Both cities grew in population and economic interdependence, symbolized in the pedestrian-railroad-highway Brownsville and Matamoros ("B&M") International Bridge bridge opened in 1910, another in 1928 called appropriately Gateway International Bridge, and telephone connection in 1929.

Capitalizing on prohibition in the United States, Matamoros established a thriving international entertainment industry (saloons, restaurants, racetracks, bullfights) to supplement a growing agricultural prosperity. Indeed, in the post-World War II years Matamoros became the celebrated locus of Mexico's cotton production, cotton gins, and cottonseed oil plants and warehouses, mirroring the success similarly enjoyed in Texas. Agricultural success eventually would give way to commerce and international industrial development, significantly the *maquiladora* or "twin-plant" system (the Border Industrial Program), for which Matamoros was chosen—quite naturally—to model as a pilot city. The four-lane Los Indios Free Trade Bridge (Puente Lucio Blanco-Los Indios) was completed in 1992, and another, the massive Veterans International Bridge (Puente Internacional Ignacio Zaragoza, honoring the Goliad-born hero of Cinco de Mayo) in 1999. Nurturing international tourism, Matamoros also enjoyed increased intercontinental trade under the North American Free Trade Agreement, the latest version of Zona Libre. Despite the various challenges of illegal immigration, drug smuggling, drug cartel violence, and other issues, the bridge-building between nations continues, connecting world powers, cultures both related and alien, and people whose ancestors were both enemies and family. Indeed, the weeklong Charro Days Fiesta, with its "positive message of international friendship, shared heritage and welcome" cosponsored by Matamoros and Brownsville, celebrated its seventy-fifth anniversary in 2012.[13] Even as Americans tend to forget the old wounds forged in the creation of Heroic Matamoros as *La Gran Puerta de México,* matamorenses, from long experience, know the risks of American capital and consumer culture are formidable, even as they indulge in them. In assessing this situation, Ramón Eduardo Ruiz aptly summarizes the entire history of Matamoros as symbolic of Mexico itself—"It is risky business to gamble your well-being on foreigners."[14] Yet it is also worth remembering how sojourners long ago, having traversed the thorny chaparral wilderness to gaze upon Matamoros on the banks of the wild Río Bravo, expressed uninhibited delight in the promise of what they perceived. This power of Matamoros to stir the imagination drove not only Mexican national policy but also the Texas Revolution and American intervention. The monumental sculpture by Sebastian now dominating the Matamoros skyline beckons this power anew—even if "exposed to all winds."

NOTES

Note to readers: Quotations throughout the text retain original spellings as found, but reprinted without the intrusive [*sic*], which can be distracting.

Chapter 1

[1] Dr. Antonio Lafon, "Report on the Yellow Fever in the City of Matamoras from September 1853 to January 1854," in *Report of the Sanitary Commission of New Orleans on the Epidemic Yellow Fever of 1853,* by the New Orleans Sanitary Commission, authorized by the New Orleans City Council (New Orleans: Picayune Office, 1854), 136.

[2] I am using the term *norteños* specifically to mean the Spanish Mexican settlers in the Villas del Norte on the lower Rio Grande, as per Omar S. Valerio-Jiménez, "Neglected Citizens and Willing Traders: The Villas del Norte (Tamaulipas) in Mexico's Northern Borderlands, 1749–1846," *Mexican Studies/Estudios Mexicanos* 18 (Summer 2002): 251–96, and Oscar J. Martínez, "The Mexican Northern Frontier, 1800–1821," *The Handbook of Hispanic Cultures: History,* ed. Alfredo Jiménez (Houston: Arte Público Press, 1994), 261–62.

[3] The misspelling is the fault of the translator or the New Orleans Sanitary Commission, not Doctor Lafon, who would have known better. "Matamoras" was the most common misspelling for more than a century in American and even British, German, and French publications.

[4] John Henry Brown, *History of Texas, from 1685 to 1892* (2 vols.; St. Louis: L. E. Daniell, 1892), I, 542.

[5] Craig H. Roell, "Matamoros Expedition of 1835–36," in Ron Tyler, Douglas E. Barnett, Roy R. Barkley, Penelope C. Anderson, and Mark F. Odintz (eds.), *The New Handbook of Texas,* (6 vols.; Austin: Texas State Historical Association, 1996), IV, 561–65; Craig H. Roell, *Remember Goliad! A History of La Bahía* (Austin: Texas State Historical Association, 1994).

[6] See, for example, D. W. C. Baker, *A Brief History of Texas from Its Earliest Settlement . . . for Schools* (New York: A. S. Barnes & Co., 1873); Mary Mitchell Brown, *A Condensed History of Texas for Schools, Prepared from the General History of John Henry Brown* (Dallas: [n.p.], 1895); Mollie Evelyn Moore Davis, *Under Six Flags: The Story of Texas* (Boston: Ginn & Co., 1897); Anna J. Hardwicke Pennybacker, *A History of Texas for Schools, Also for General Reading and for Teachers Preparing Themselves for Examination* (Tyler, Tex: [n.p.], 1888; 1895; rev. eds.; Austin: Mrs. Percy V. Pennybacker, 1908; 1912; 1924); Katie Daffan, *Texas Heroes: An Historical Reader for the Grades* (Boston: Benj. H. Sanborn & Co., 1908); and John Rosenfield Jr. with Jack Patton, *Texas History Movies* (Dallas: P. L. Turner Co, 1928; rev. ed.; Dallas: Magnolia Petroleum Co., 1943; 1954).

[7] Jack Jackson to Tim O'Shea, interview, *Silver Bullet Comic Books* (n.d.), <http://www.comicsbulletin.com/news/107120924726012.htm> [Accessed Sept. 6, 2008]. Jackson was commenting on his *The Alamo: An Epic Told from Both Sides* (Austin: Paisano Graphics, 2002).

[8] Recent books that discuss this fascinating literature are Walter Buenger and Robert A. Calvert (eds.), *Texas Through Time: Evolving Interpretations* (College Station: Texas A&M University Press, 1991); Laura Lyons McLemore, *Inventing Texas: Early Historians of the Lone Star State* (College Station: Texas A&M University Press, 2004); and Gregg Cantrell and Elizabeth Hayes (eds.), *Lone Star Pasts: Memory and History in Texas* (College Station: Texas A&M University Press, 2007).

[9] Andrés Reséndez, *Changing National Identities at the Frontier: Texas and New Mexico, 1800–1850* (Cambridge, UK: Cambridge University Press, 2005), 150.

[10] For an American perspective on the role of Manifest Destiny in the Texas story, see Frederick Merk, *Manifest Destiny and Mission in American History: A Reinterpretation* (New York: Vintage Books, 1963); David M. Pletcher, *The Diplomacy of Annexation: Texas, Oregon, and the Mexican War* (Columbia: University of Missouri Press, 1973); and Robert E. May, *Manifest Destiny's Underworld: Filibustering in Antebellum America* (Chapel Hill: University of North Carolina Press, 2002). For a Mexican perspective, see Gene M. Brack, *Mexico Views Manifest Destiny, 1821–1846: An Essay on the Origins of the Mexican War* (Albuquerque: University of New Mexico Press, 1975); Gáston García Cantú, *Las invasiones norteamericanos en México* (México, D.F.: Fonda de Cultura Económica y Secretaría de la Defensa Naciónal, 1996); and María del Rosario Rodríguez Díaz, "Mexico's Vision of Manifest Destiny during the 1847 War," *Journal of Popular Culture* 35 (Fall 2001): 41–50. For a critique of Manifest Destiny from a German perspective, see Andreas Reichstein, *Rise of the Lone Star: The Making of Texas,* trans. Jeanne R. Willson (College Station: Texas A&M University Press, 1989). For a British perspective especially significant to Matamoros, see Stuart Reid, *The Secret War for Texas* (College Station: Texas A&M University Press, 2007).

[11] For example, Jesús F. de la Teja (ed.), *Tejano Leadership in Mexican and Revolutionary Texas* (College Station: Texas A&M University Press, 2010); David J. Weber, *The Mexican Frontier, 1821–1846: The American Southwest under Mexico* (Albuquerque: University of New Mexico Press, 1982); Andrés Tijerina, *Tejanos and Texas under the Mexican Flag, 1821–1836* (College Station: Texas A&M University Press, 1994); Jesús F. de la Teja, "The Colonization and Independence of Texas: A Tejano Perspective," in *Myths, Misdeeds, and Misunderstandings: The Roots of Conflict in United States-Mexico Relations*, eds. Jaime E. Rodríguez O. and Kathryn Vincent (Wilmington, Del: Scholarly Resources, 1997), 79–95; and Omar S. Valerio-Jiménez, *River of Hope: Forging Identity and Nation in the Rio Grande Borderlands* (Durham, N.C.: Duke University Press, 2013).

[12] See Stephen L. Hardin, *Texian Iliad: A Military History of the Texas Revolution, 1835–1836* (Austin: University of Texas Press, 1994); Paul D. Lack, *The Texas Revolutionary Experience: A Political and Social History, 1835–1836* (College Station: Texas A&M University Press, 1996); Randy Roberts and James S. Olson, *A Line in the Sand: The Alamo in Blood and Memory* (New York: Free Press, 2001); William C. Davis, *Lone Star Rising: The Revolutionary Birth of the Texas Republic* (New York: Free Press, 2003); H. W. Brands, *Lone Star Nation: The Epic Story of the Battle for Texas Independence* (New York: Random House, 2004); James E. Crisp, *Sleuthing the Alamo: Davy Crockett's Last Stand and Other Mysteries of the Texas Revolution* (New York: Oxford University Press, 2004); Edward L. Miller, *New Orleans and the Texas Revolution* (College Station: Texas A&M University Press, 2004); and Will Fowler, *Santa Anna of Mexico* (Lincoln: University of Nebraska Press, 2008).

[13] José Enrique de la Peña, *With Santa Anna in Texas: A Personal Narrative of the Revolution*, trans. Carmen Perry (rev. ed.; College Station: Texas A&M University Press, 1997), xxx.

[14] Excellent Mexican resources for the history of Matamoros (some available at <http://matamoros.com.mx>) are Arturo Zárate-Ruiz, *Matamoros: Textos y pretextos de identidad. Su historia, terrirorio, cultura y comida* (Ciudad Victoria: El Colegio de Tamaulipas, 2005); José Raúl Canseco Botello, *História de Matamoros* (2nd ed.; H. Matamoros, Tamaulipas: Tipográficos de

Litográfica Jardín, 1981); Andrés F. Cuellar, *Cronología Histórica de Matamoros* (H. Matamoros, Tamaulipas: Archivo Histórico Casamata, [n.d.]); and Clemente Rendón de la Garza, *Bicentenario de Nuestra Señora del Refugio de los Esteros Catedral, H. Matamoros, Tamaulipas, México* (H. Matamoros, Tamaulipas: [n.p.], 1994). See also Eliseo Paredes Manzano, *Homenaje a los fundadores de la Heróica, Leal e invicta Matamoros en la sesquicentenario de su nuevo nombre* (H. Matamoros, Tamaulipas: Ayuntamiento de Matamoros, 1976); Andrés F. Cuéllar, *De Matamoros a México con sus gobernantes* (H. Matamoros, Tamaulipas: Ediciones Archivo Histórico, 1996); Clemente Rendón de la Garza, *Vidas ilustres en la historia y la cultura de la Heróica Matamoros* (Monterrey, Nuevo León: Grafo Print Editores, 2000); Oscar Rivera Saldaña, *Diccionario Biográfico de la Heróica Matamoros* (H. Matamoros, Tamaulipas: Librería Española, 2001); and Octavio Herrera, *Breve historia de Tamaulipas* (México, D.F.: El Colegio de México, Fideicomiso de Historia de las Américas, Fondo de Cultura Económica, 1999). For the Mexican side of border issues, the studies and publications of the Colegio de la Frontera Norte (El Colef) are unsurpassed and may be accessed at <http://www.colef.mx/>.

[15] Arturo Zárate-Ruiz, "Not Spotty, Not Tidy: Matamoros, the Threshold of Life," August 13, 2004, <http://www.matamoros.com> [Accessed Sept. 29, 2007] (pdf document in author's possession); Octavio Herrera Pérez, historian and founder of El Colegio de Tamaulipas, is quoted at "Matamoros: La Gran Puerta de México," <http://www.lagranpuertademexico.com/inicio.htm> [Accessed July 21, 2008]; "Parque Cultural Olímpico," Un vistazo a Matamoros, <http://www.ocvmatamoros.com.mx/por-la-ciudad-1.htm> [Accessed Aug. 28, 2011]; Ivonne Ma. Martínez Cadena (ed.), *H. Matamoros, Tamaulipas: la gran puerta de Mexico* (2nd ed.; Matamoros, Tamaulipas: Ink Servicios Gráficos, 2006).

[16] Mary Jo Galindo, "Con Un Pie En Cada Lado: Ethnicities and the Archaeology of Spanish Colonial Ranching Communities along the Lower Río Grande Valley" (PhD diss., University of Texas at Austin 2003), ix.

[17] This overview of Matamoros's history in this and successive paragraphs is collected from the excellent resources listed in note 14 above, particularly the works of Arturo Zárate-Ruiz, José Raúl Canseco Botello, Andrés F. Cuellar, Clemente Rendón de la Garza, and Oscar Rivera Saldaña.

[18] Other municipalities in Tamaulipas renamed in 1826–28 after heroes of independence include Villa de Bustamante, Villa de Morelos, Villa de Hidalgo, Villa de Jiménez. "Estado de Tamaulipas," *La Enciclopedia de los Municipios de México*, <http://www.e-local.gob.mx/work/templates/enciclo/tamaulipas/> [Accessed Aug. 26, 2011].

[19] Miguel de Cervantes Saavedra, *Don Quixote: History and Adventures*, trans. Tobias George Smollett (Ware, UK: Wordsworth Editions, 1998), 831–32, 833.

[20] Milo Kearney and Manuel Medrano, *Medieval Culture and the Mexican American Borderlands* (College Station: Texas A&M University Press, 2001), 1, 103.

[21] Thomas Bangs Thorpe, *Our Army on the Rio Grande: Being a Short Account of the Important Events Transpiring from the Time of the Removal of the "Army of Occupation" from Corpus Christi, to the Surrender of Matamoros . . .* (Philadelphia: Carey and Hart, 1846), 129.

[22] "La Conformación de Matamoros: Fortificaciones," Historia de H. Matamoros, <http://75.125.212.253/matamoros/historia/conformacion.php> [Accessed Aug. 26, 2011]; Andres Florentino Cuellar, "Casamata," <http://blue.utb.edu/localhistory/CASAMATA.htm> [Accessed Aug. 26, 2011]; "Juan Nepomuceno Molano," *Nuevo Diccionario Biográfico de la Heroica Matamoros*, <http://soctamdehistoria.org/db/letraM/Molano_Juan_Nepomuceno.htm> [Accessed Aug. 26, 2011]; Eliseo Paredes Manzano, *La Casa Mata y fortificaciones de la heróica Matamoros, Tamaulipas* (H. Matamoros, Tamaulipas: [n.p.], 1974).

[23] Thomas B. Carroll, "Heroica Matamoros, Tamaulipas, Mexico: Where Were the Fortifications of the Walled City?" in *Studies in Brownsville and Matamoros History*, ed. Milo Kearney, Anthony Knopp, and Antonio Zavaleta (Brownsville: University of Texas at Brownsville and

Texas Southmost College, 1995), 75–122. In addition to this volume, the team of Kearney, Knopp, and more recently Zavaleta has produced an excellent series of mostly English-language books specific to the history of Matamoros. See Milo Kearney and Anthony K. Knopp, *Boom and Bust: The Historical Cycles of Matamoros and Brownsville* (Austin: Eakin Press, 1992); Milo Kearney and Anthony Knopp, *Border Cuates: A History of the U.S.-Mexican Twin Cities* (Austin: Eakin Press, 1995); Milo Kearney, Anthony K. Knopp, and Antonio Zavaleta (eds.), *Studies in Matamoros and Cameron County History* (Brownsville: University of Texas at Brownsville and Texas Southmost College, 1997); Milo Kearney, Anthony K. Knopp, and Antonio Zavaleta (eds.), *Studies in Rio Grande Valley History* (Brownsville: University of Texas at Brownsville and Texas Southmost College, 2005); Milo Kearney, Anthony Knopp, and Antonio Zavaleta (eds.), *More Studies in Rio Grande Valley History* (Brownsville: University of Texas at Brownsville and Texas Southmost College, 2006); Milo Kearney, Anthony Knopp, and Antonio Zavaleta (eds.), *Additional Studies in Rio Grande Valley History* (Brownsville: University of Texas at Brownsville, 2008); Milo Kearney, Anthony Knopp, and Antonio Zavaleta (eds.), *Continuing Studies in Rio Grande Valley History* (Brownsville: Texas Center for Border and Transnational Studies, University of Texas at Brownsville, 2010); Milo Kearney, Anthony Knopp, and Antonio Zavaleta (eds.), *Ongoing Studies in Rio Grande Valley History* (Brownsville: Texas Center for Border and Transnational Studies, University of Texas at Brownsville, 2011). For an excellent overview, see Mary Margaret McAllen Amberson, James A. McAllen, Margaret H. McAllen, *I Would Rather Sleep in Texas: A History of the Lower Rio Grande Valley and the People of the Santa Anita Land Grant* (Austin: Texas State Historical Association, 2003).

[24] Jean Louis Berlandier, *Journey to Mexico During the Years 1826 to 1834* (2 vols.; Austin: Texas State Historical Association, 1980), II, 433, 518.

[25] David Montejano, *Anglos and Mexicans in the Making of Texas, 1836–1986* (Austin: University of Texas Press, 1987), 16; Consulate General of the United States: Matamoros, Mexico <http://matamoros.usconsulate.gov/about_the_consulate.html> [Accessed Aug. 26, 2011].

[26] Creed Taylor, "Dr. Grant and His Matamoros Expedition Starts Trouble," Sons of DeWitt Colony Texas, <http://www.tamu.edu/ccbn/dewitt/goliadcreed.htm> [Accessed Aug. 26, 2011].

[27] A Texian, *Mexico versus Texas, a Descriptive Novel* (Philadelphia N. Siegried, 1838), 192; William Kennedy, *Texas: The Rise, Progress, and Prospects of the Republic of Texas* (2 vols.; London: R. Hastings, 1841), I:57–58.

[28] Graham Davis, *Land! Irish Pioneers in Mexican and Revolutionary Texas* (College Station: Texas A&M University Press, 2002), 129; Aaron Morton Sakolski, *The Great American Land Bubble: The Amazing Story of Land-Grabbing, Speculations, and Booms from Colonial Days to the Present Time* (New York: Harper, 1932), 213–31.

[29] The Mexican federal Congress passed the national colonization law on August 18, 1824. Based on this, Coahuila y Texas passed its own state colonization law on March 25, 1825. Among other things, the national law forbade land grants within twenty leagues of an international boundary or within ten leagues of the coast without federal permission. Further, Congress reserved the right to stop immigration from particular nations in the interest of national security—a clause aimed specifically at the United States.

[30] Zárate-Ruiz, *Matamoros,* 44.

[31] See chapter 2, "Empresarios," in Roell, *Remember Goliad!*; Roell, "Plácido Benavides," *The New Handbook of Texas*, I, 484; and Roell, "De León's Colony," *The New Handbook of Texas*, II, 573–74. For an extended treatment, see Ana Carolina Castillo Crimm, *De León: A Tejano Family History* (Austin: University of Texas Press, 2004). See also Stephen L. Hardin, "Plácido Benavides: Fighting Tejano Federalist," in De la Teja (ed.), *Tejano Leadership in Mexican and Revolutionary Texas*, 56–75; and Crimm, "Fernando De León, Leadership Lost," in De la Teja (ed.), *Tejano Leadership in Mexican and Revolutionary Texas*, 102–27.

[32] Graham Davis, "Land and Freedom: The Irish in the Texas Revolution," *REDEN: Revista Espanola de Estudios Norteamericanos* 7, no. 12 (1996), <http://www.bathspa.ac.uk/schools/humanities-and-cultural-industries/irish-studies/research-projects/reden.pdf>, 81–96 [Accessed Aug. 20, 2008].

Chapter 2

[1] McClintock was a volunteer in the Second Kentucky Regiment serving in the United States-Mexican War. William A. McClintock, "Journal of a Trip through Texas and Northern Mexico in 1846–1847," *Southwestern Historical Quarterly Online* 34 (January 1931): 231.

[2] George C. Furber, *The Twelve Months Volunteer: Or, Journal of a Private, in the Tennessee Regiment of Cavalry, in the Campaign, in Mexico, 1846–7* (Cincinnati: J. A. & U. P. James, 1848), 165–66, 183–85, 296–97.

[3] Frederick Adolph Wislizenus, *Memoir of a Tour to Northern Mexico: Connected with Col. Doniphan's Expedition, in 1846 and 1847* (Washington, D.C.: Tippin & Streepers, 1848), 36; Frederick Law Olmsted, *A Journey Through Texas; Or, A Saddle-trip on the Southwestern Frontier* (New York: Dix, Edwards & Co., 1857), 453

[4] Thomas Meade Harwell, *Studies in Texan Folklore—Rio Grande Valley: Twelve Folklore Studies with Introductions, Commentaries & a Bounty of Notes* (Lewiston, N.Y.: Edwin Mellen Press, 1997), 145.

[5] Manuel Mier y Terán, *Texas by Terán: The Diary Kept by General Manuel de Mier y Terán on His 1828 Inspection of Texas*, ed. Jack Jackson and trans. John Wheat (Austin: University of Texas Press, 2000), 165; William B. Dewees, Jan. 6, 1827, in William B. Dewees, *Letters from an Early Settler of Texas*, comp. Cara Cardelle [Emmaretta Cara Kimball Crawford] (2nd ed.; Louisville, Ky.: New Albany Tribune, 1858), 63–64.

[6] John C. Duval, *Early Times in Texas* (Austin: Gammel, 1892), 27; Ulysses Simpson Grant, *Personal Memoirs of U. S. Grant* (2 vols.; New York: Charles L. Webster & Co., 1885), I, 87. The standard works on the wild mustangs of the Trans-Nueces country are Jack Jackson, *Los Mesteños: Spanish Ranching in Texas, 1721–1821* (College Station: Texas A&M University Press, 1986); Don Worcester, *The Spanish Mustang* (El Paso: Texas Western Press, 1986); and J. Frank Dobie, *The Mustangs* (Boston: Little, Brown, 1952).

[7] Berlandier, *Journey to Mexico*, 542–49, 569–72.

[8] William Watson, *The Adventures of a Blockade Runner: Or, Trade in Time of War* (London: T. F. Unwin: 1893), 16, 18, 23; Furber, *The Twelve Months Volunteer*, 191–92; Kearney and Knopp, *Boom and Bust*, 42.

[9] Furber, *The Twelve Months Volunteer*, 186; Thorpe, *Our Army on the Rio Grande*, 130; William Seaton Henry, *Campaign Sketches of the War with Mexico* (New York: Harper & Brothers, 1847), 65.

[10] Thorpe, *Our Army on the Rio Grande*, 131, 136, 139; John Frost, *The Mexican War and Its Warriors: Comprising a Complete History of All the Operations of the American Armies in Mexico* (New Haven, Conn.: H. Mansfield, 1848), 59–60; Furber, *The Twelve Months Volunteer*, 189–90.

[11] Furber, *The Twelve Months Volunteer*, 188–89.

[12] Furber, *The Twelve Months Volunteer*, 189.

[13] Frost, *The Mexican War and Its Warriors*, 60; Furber, *The Twelve Months Volunteer*, 189, 190; Thorpe, *Our Army on the Rio Grande*, 136.

[14] Furber, *The Twelve Months Volunteer*, 213–14.

[15] Lafon, "Report on Yellow Fever in the City of Matamoras," 136.

Chapter 3

[1] Leroy P. Graf, "The Economic History of the Lower Rio Grande Valley, 1820–1875" (PhD diss., Harvard University, 1942), 93 (Smith quotation); Montejano, *Anglos and Mexicans in the Making of Texas*, 16, 18 (Smith quotation).

[2] Patricia Osante, *Orígenes del Nuevo Santander, 1748–1772* (México, D.F.: Universidad Nacional Autónoma de México, 1997), 143, 179; Omar S. Valerio-Jiménez, "Neglected Citizens and Willing Traders: The Villas del Norte (Tamaulipas) in Mexico's Northern Borderlands, 1749–1846," *Mexican Studies/Estudios Mexicanos* 18 (Summer 2002): 252–55; Armando C. Alonzo, "A History of Ranching in Nuevo Santander's Villas del Norte, 1730s–1848," in *Coastal Encounters: The Transformation of the Gulf South in the Eighteenth Century*, ed. Richmond F. Brown (Lincoln: University of Nebraska Press, 2008), 195, 208. See also John A. Adams, *Conflict and Commerce on the Rio Grande: Laredo, 1755–1955* (College Station: Texas A&M University Press, 2008).

[3] Weber, *The Mexican Frontier*, 240, 284; Valerio-Jiménez, "Neglected Citizens and Willing Traders," 262.

[4] Galindo, "Con Un Pie En Cada Lado," 309–10; Valerio-Jiménez, "Neglected Citizens and Willing Traders," 265–66.

[5] Canseco Botello, *Historía de Matamoros*, 70.

[6] Canseco Botello, *Historía de Matamoros*, 19; Zárate-Ruiz, *Matamoros*, 34.

[7] See Jackson, *Los Mesteños*; Montejano, *Anglos and Mexicans in the Making of Texas*; Joe S. Graham, *El Rancho in South Texas: Continuity and Change from 1750* (Denton: University of North Texas Press, 1994); Jerry D. Thompson, *A Wild and Vivid Land: An Illustrated History of the South Texas Border* (Austin: Texas State Historical Association, 1997); Jaime E. Rodríguez O. and Kathryn Vincent (eds.), *Myths, Misdeeds, and Misunderstandings: The Roots of Conflict in U.S.-Mexican Relations* (Wilmington, Del.: Scholarly Resources, 1997); Andrés Tijerina, *Tejano Empire: Life on the South Texas Ranchos* (College Station: Texas A&M University Press, 1998); Elena Zamora O'Shea, *El Mesquite: A Story of the Early Spanish Settlements between the Nueces and the Rio Grande* (College Station: Texas A&M University Press, 2000); Daniel David Arreola, *Tejano South Texas: A Mexican American Cultural Province* (University of Texas Press, 2002); Davis, *Land!*; and Reséndez, *Changing National Identities at the Frontier*.

[8] See Roell, *Remember Goliad!*, and Castillo Crimm, *De León*.

[9] Juan Mora-Torres, *The Making of the Mexican Border: The State, Capitalism, and Society in Nuevo Leon, 1848–1910* (Austin: University of Texas Press, 2001), 30; Charles A. Hale, *El liberalismo mexicano en la época de Mora* (México, D.F.: Siglo XXI, 1999), 81.

[10] Zárate-Ruiz, *Matamoros*, 20; Pat Kelley, *River of Lost Dreams: Navigation on the Rio Grande* (Lincoln: University of Nebraska Press, 1986), 18–22.

[11] José María Quirós, *Memoria de estatuto* (Veracruz, 1817), in Jaime E. Rodríguez O., *Down from Colonialism: Mexico's Nineteenth-Century Crisis* (Los Angeles: Chicano Studies Research Center Publications, University of California at Los Angeles, 1983), at the Historical Text Archive, <http://historicaltextarchive.com/sections.php?action=read&artid=528> [Accessed Aug. 26, 2011].

[12] The name of Tamaulipas, as the official state website puts it, is the subject of "a very heated controversy among historians" ("*es tema de una polémica muy acalorada entre los historiadores*"). Taken from *tamaholipa*, a Huastec term, the prefix *tam-* signifies "place where," but scholars disagree on the meaning of *holipa*. "High mountains" or "high hills" is a common interpretation, dating to 1792 with Fray Vicente de Santa María's understanding of the native phrasing. A newer interpretation advocates that it means "place of much praying," with others suggesting "where the Lipan pray," the latter more controversial because it begs the question of northern Lipan ancestry (*descendientes de los norteños lipanes*). Still another view is "place of the Olives," a reference to the Olive Indians (*un grupo de indígenas olives*) brought "very far to the north" in 1544 by the renowned evangelist, linguist, and chronicler, Fray Andrés de Olmos, to resettle in what he called "Tamaholipa," with "olipa" a distortion of Olive (*olipa, deformación de olive*). See Gobierno de Tamaulipas, Historia, <http://tamaulipas.gob.mx/tamaulipas/historia/> [Accessed Aug. 26, 2011]; Instituto Nacional Para el Federalismo y el Desarrollo Municipal, Reseña Histórica de las Entidades Federativas (Secretaría

de Gobernación, Archivo General de la Nación, "El Federalismo Mexicano," México 1996), 34, <http://www.inafed.gob.mx/work/resources/DocInt2006/ResenaHistoricadelasEntidadesFederativas.pdf> [Accessed Aug. 13, 2008]; Eugenio del Hoyo, *Historia del Nuevo Reino de León, 1577–1723* (Monterrey, Nuevo León: Instituto Tecnológico y de Estudios Superiores, 1972), 10.

[13] Moreover, the wealthier *ciudadanos* in Matamoros held political and civil rights, while poorer *paisanos* retained only civil rights. Foreigners and Indians at best had very restricted rights and could not participate in the political system—although certain foreign merchants who provided a long-standing and valuable service to the community, received political privileges, such as serving in trials involving fellow immigrants. Jean Berlandier was thus "an exceptional case of a foreigner who managed to hold a lower-level public office." Valerio-Jiménez, "Neglected Citizens and Willing Traders," 275–80; William H. Beezley and David E. Lorey (eds.), *Viva Mexico! Viva La Independencia! Celebrations of September 16* (Wilmington, Del.: Scholarly Resources, 2000), 79–82. See also Andrés Reséndez, "National Identity on a Shifting Border: Texas and New Mexico in the Age of Transition, 1821–1848," *Journal of American History* 86 (September 1999): 668–88.

[14] Zárate-Ruiz, *Matamoros,* 40; Cuellar, *Cronología Histórica de Matamoros,* 11; Herrera, *Breve historia de Tamaulipas,* 128; Armondo C. Alonzo, *Tejano Legacy: Rancheros and Settlers in South Texas, 1734–1900* (Albuquerque: University of New Mexico Press, 1998), 78–79. Despite an economic downturn caused primarily by revolution in Texas, customs house tonnage duty for Matamoros by 1841 translated into $279,627 net proceeds after deducting the costs of collection, which measures an impressive $2.58 billion in current value (2011), offering clear evidence of the continuing allure of Matamoros. See "Commerce and Resources of Mexico," *The Merchants' Magazine and Commercial Review* 10 (January–June 1844): 128. The inflation-adjusted figure of current value was calculated at www.MeasuringWorth.com.

[15] "Commerce and Resources of Mexico," *The Merchants' Magazine and Commercial Review* 10 (January–June 1844): 128, 130.

[16] Valerio-Jiménez, "Neglected Citizens and Willing Traders," 281.

[17] Valerio-Jiménez, "Neglected Citizens and Willing Traders," 265–67; George Francis Lyon, *Journal of a Residence and Tour in the Republic of Mexico in the Year 1826: With Some Account of the Mines of that Country* (London: John Murray, 1828), 36; Galindo, "Con Un Pie En Cada Lado," 309–10; Canseco Botello, *Historia de Matamoros,* 70.

[18] Alonzo, *Tejano Legacy,* 67–73; Graf, "The Economic History of the Lower Rio Grande Valley," 52–55, 110–11, 117; Weber, *The Mexican Frontier,* 151; Valerio-Jiménez, "Neglected Citizens and Willing Traders," 282–83.

[19] Furber, *Twelve Month Volunteer,* 371n–75n; Josiah Gregg, *Commerce of the Prairies: Or, The Journal of a Santa Fé Trader, During Eight Expeditions Across the Great Western Prairies, and a Residence of Nearly Nine Years in Northern Mexico* (2 vols.; New York: H. G. Langley, 1844; 5th ed., Philadelphia: J. W. Moore, 1851), I, 112, 180–84; II, 162

[20] The Mexican government's commitment was confirmed when the Texas provisional government sent officers to Matamoros to reclaim runaway slaves in 1836. Matamoros authorities concealed the ex-slaves and the Texans were arrested and then returned home empty-handed. See John C. Gassner, "African American Fugitive Slaves and Freemen in Matamoros, Tamaulipas, 1820–1865" (M.A. thesis, University of Texas-Pan American, 2003); Ronnie C. Tyler, "Fugitive Slaves in Mexico," *The Journal of Negro History* 57 (January, 1972): 1–12; Rosalie Schwartz, *Across the Rio to Freedom: U.S. Negroes in Mexico* (El Paso: Texas Western Press, 1975); and Arturo Zárate-Ruiz, "Fugitive Slaves and Free Blacks in South Texas," in Kearney, Knopp, and Zavaleta (eds.), *Further Studies in Rio Grande Valley History.* On slavery in Texas, see Alwyn Barr, *Black Texans: A History of African Americans in Texas, 1528–1995* (2nd ed.; Norman: University of Oklahoma Press, 1996); Randolph B. Campbell, *An Empire for*

Slavery: The Peculiar Institution in Texas, 1821–1865 (Baton Rouge: Louisiana State University Press, 1989); Paul D. Lack, "Slavery and the Texas Revolution," *Southwestern Historical Quarterly* 89 (October 1985): 181–202; and Josefina Zoraida Vázquez, "The Colonization and Loss of Texas: A Mexican Perspective," in Rodríguez O. and Vincent (eds.), *Myths, Misdeeds, and Misunderstandings: The Roots of Conflict in U.S.-Mexican Relations*, 47–77.

   [21] Juan N. Almonte, *Almonte's Texas: Juan N. Almonte's 1834 Inspection, Secret Report, and Role in the 1836 Campaign*, ed. Jack Jackson and trans. John Wheat (Austin: Texas State Historical Association, 2004), 54.

   [22] Simón Tadeo Ortiz de Ayala, *México considerado como nación independiente y libre, ó sean, Algunas indicaciones sobre los deberes más esenciales de los mexicanos* ([n.p.]: Imprenta de Carlos Lawalle Sobrino, 1832), 374, 430, 594.

   [23] Juan N. Almonte, "Statistical Report on Texas," trans. Carlos E. Castañeda, *Southwestern Historical Quarterly* 28 (January 1925): 178, 179, 193.

   [24] Almonte, *Almonte's Texas*, 227.

   [25] Mora-Torres, *Making of the Mexican Border*, 30–31.

   [26] Zárate-Ruiz, *Matamoros*, 44; Valerio-Jiménez, "Neglected Citizens and Willing Traders," 284–85, 287–88; Miller, *New Orleans and the Texas Revolution*, 91.

   [27] Weber, *The Mexican Frontier*, 146.

Chapter 4

   [1] Stephen F. Austin to President of Consultation, in Eugene C. Barker (ed.), *The Austin Papers* (3 vols.; Washington, DC: U.S. Government Printing Office, 1924–28), III, 240.

   [2] There is debate on the Indian origins of the word that the Spaniards transliterated into *huracán*. Louis A. Perez Jr., *Winds of Change: Hurricanes and the Transformation of Nineteenth-Century Cuba* (Chapel Hill: University of North Carolina Press, 2000), 17–19; Kerry Emanuel, *Divine Wind: The History and Science of Hurricanes* (New York: Oxford University Press, 2005), 18–21; Kay Almere Read and Jason J. González, *Mesoamerican Mythology: A Guide to the Gods, Heroes, Rituals, and Beliefs of Mexico and Central America* (New York: Oxford University Press, 2000), 200; Héctor Cuevas Fernández and Mario Havarrete Hernández, "Los hurcanes en la época prehispánica y en el siglo XVI," 39–40, <http://www.uv.mx/eventos/inundaciones2005/PDF/03_HURACANES.pdf> [Accessed Jan. 3, 2012].

   [3] William C. Redfield, *On Three Several Hurricanes of the Atlantic, and Their Relations to the Northers of Mexico and Central America: And Their Relations to the Northers of Mexico and Central America, with Notices of Other Storms* (New Haven, Conn.: B. L. Hamlen, 1846), 31–32. The very destructive Racer's Storm first hit Kingston, Jamaica, before eventually hitting Tampico, then Matamoros, and continued along the Gulf Coast, hitting Galveston, New Orleans, and then West Florida, before climbing to both Carolinas and finally heading into the Atlantic Ocean.

   [4] Fowler provocatively demonstrates that Santa Anna's Plan of Cuernavaca and swift move against the radical reforms of Congress had the backing of the church, the army, the more powerful sectors of society, as well as enormous popular support. As "a federalist, a republican, and, ultimately, a moderate liberal," Santa Anna was not opposed to reform so much as he took issue with the pace of reform. Moreover, despite the opportunity, Santa Anna did not seize draconian power and believed he was actually saving his country by preventing extremists from coming into power—enemies bearing grudges birthed during the war for Mexican independence. Fowler, *Santa Anna of Mexico*, 154–56.

   [5] Fowler, *Santa Anna of Mexico*, 159. Emphasis in the original.

   [6] See Miller, *New Orleans and the Texas Revolution*, 27–36, 58, 86–92, 104.

   [7] Vázquez, "Colonization and Loss of Texas," 66.

   [8] Miller, *New Orleans and the Texas Revolution*, 3, 4 (quotation). 36, 62.

[9] Valerio-Jiménez, "Neglected Citizens and Willing Traders," 289, 291

[10] Berlandier, *Indians of Texas*, 6, 122–23.

[11] Berlandier, *Indians of Texas*, 119; Pekka Hamalainen, *The Comanche Empire* (New Haven, Conn.: Yale University Press, 2008), 198–99, 221; Foster Todd Smith, *From Dominance to Disappearance: The Indians of Texas and the Near Southwest, 1786–1859* (Lincoln: University of Nebraska Press, 2005), 137, 144; Thomas W. Kavanagh, *The Comanches: A History, 1706–1875* (Lincoln: University of Nebraska Press, 1999), 249.

[12] *El Ancla* 1, no. 36 (June 8, 1838), quoted in Valerio-Jiménez, "Neglected Citizens and Willing Traders," 137.

[13] See Paul D. Lack, "Consultation"; Ralph W. Steen, "Provisional Government" and "General Council"; and "Declaration of November 7, 1835," *The Handbook of Texas Online*, <http://www.tshaonline.org/handbook/online/articles/mjc08>, <http://www.tshaonline.org/handbook/online/articles/mzp01>, <http://www.tshaonline.org/handbook/online/articles/mbg01> and <http://www.tshaonline.org/handbook/online/articles/mjd02> [Accessed Nov. 16, 2012].

[14] Dimmitt to Austin, Nov. 14, 1835, in Barker (ed.), *Austin Papers*, III, 253; Dimmitt to Austin, Oct. 15, 1835, in Barker (ed.), *Austin Papers*, III, 185–86; Dimmitt to [?], Dec. 2, 1835, in John Holmes Jenkins (ed.), *The Papers of the Texas Revolution, 1835–1836* (10 vols.; Austin: Presidial Press, 1973), III, 77–78, hereafter cited as Jenkins (ed.), *PTR*.

[15] Hobart Huson, *Captain Phillip Dimmitt's Commandancy of Goliad* (Austin: Von Boeckmann-Jones, 1974), 155–56. See also Craig Roell, "Dimmitt, Philip," in *The New Handbook of Texas*; II, 648–50; and Roell, *Remember Goliad!*, 36–45.

[16] Dimmitt paraphrasing himself from an earlier letter to Austin, quoted in Dimmitt to Austin, Nov. 14, 1835, in Barker (ed.), *Austin Papers*, III, 252–53; Zavala recommendation in Dimmitt to [?], Dec. 2, 1835, in Jenkins (ed.), *PTR*, III, 77–78. For Dimmitt's role in the origin of the Matamoros expedition, see Huson, *Dimmitt's Commandancy of Goliad*, 153. See also Hobart Huson, *Refugio: A Comprehensive History of Refugio County from Aboriginal Times to 1953* (2 vols.; Woodsboro, Tex.: Rooke Foundation, 1953–55), I, 260.

[17] Austin to President of the Consultation, Nov. 5, 1835, in Barker (ed.), *Austin Papers*, III, 240; José Antonio Mexía to Consultation (trans. by Zavala), Oct. 29, 1835, in Jenkins (ed.), *PTR*, II, 262–64. Huson, *Dimmitt's Commandancy of Goliad*, 161–64; Zavala to Dimmitt, Dec. 9, 1835, in Jenkins (ed.), *PTR*, III, 131.

[18] Miller, *New Orleans and the Texas Revolution*, 98, 104, 203. See 85–107 for Mexía's disaster at Tampico.

[19] Dimmitt to Austin, Nov. 14, 1835, in Barker (ed.), *Austin Papers*, III, 252–53; Dimmitt to Wyly Martin, Nov. 15, 1835, in Jenkins (ed.), *PTR*, II, 419–20.

[20] Vázquez, "Colonization and Loss of Texas," 71.

[21] Dimmitt to Public, Nov. 12, 1835, in Jenkins (ed.), *PTR*, II, 382; and Dimmitt to Austin, Nov. 13, 1835, Jenkins (ed.), *PTR*, II, 389–92; Austin to Dimmitt, Nov. 18, 1835, in Jenkins (ed.), *PTR*, II, 448; Austin to Provisional Government, Nov. 18, 1835, Jenkins (ed.), *PTR*, II, 450; Goliad Volunteers to Austin, Nov. 21, 1835, in Jenkins (ed.), *PTR*, II, 480–84. Fisher-Power quoted in *Journal of the Proceedings of the General Council of the Republic of Texas held at San Felipe de Austin, November 14th, 1835–March 11th, 1836* (Houston, 1839), 674.

Chapter 5

[1] Dimmitt to President of Convention, Nov. 29, 1835, in Jenkins (ed.), *PTR*, III, 21.

[2] Dimmitt to [?], Dec 2, 1835, in Jenkins (ed.), *PTR*, III, 77–78; Huson, *Dimmitt's Commandancy of Goliad*, 160; and Herbert Davenport, "James W. Fannin's Part in the Texas Revolution, chapter 9, Harbert Davenport Papers (manuscript; Dolph Briscoe Center for American History, University of Texas at Austin).

³ Zavala to Dimmitt, Dec. 9, 1835, in Jenkins (ed.), *PTR*, III, 131; Miller, *New Orleans and the Texas Revolution*, 97.

⁴ See Davenport, "James W. Fannin's Part in the Texas Revolution," chapter 9, as well as his "Men of Goliad," *Southwestern Historical Quarterly* 43 (July 1939): 7.

⁵ Huson, *Dimmitt's Commandancy of Goliad*, 156–58; Dianna Everett, *The Texas Cherokees: A People Between Two Fires, 1819–1840* (Norman: University of Oklahoma Press, 1995), 90–91.

⁶ Gobierno del Departmento Tamaulipas, Circular, José Antonio Fernández, Dec. 8, 1835, Dorothy Sloan Rare Books, Auction 21, Llano, Tex., Oct. 26, 2007, <http://www.dsloan.com/Auctions/A21/item-bangs-tamaulipas.html> [Accessed Aug. 26, 2011]. Even though this document was imprinted by Samuel Bangs, the official printer for the state of Tamaulipas at the time, then living in Ciudad Victoria, it is not in Lota M. Spell's or John H. Jenkins's bibliographies of Bangs's imprints, nor is it in Thomas W. Streeter's bibliography of Texas imprints, and therefore extremely rare. Apparently, according to OCLC and WorldCat.org, only Yale University has a copy.

⁷ Houston to Bowie, Dec. 17, 1835, in Eugene C. Barker and Amelia W. Williams (eds.), *The Writings of Sam Houston* (8 vols.; Austin: University of Texas Press, 1938–1943), I, 322–23; Davenport, "James W. Fannin's Part in the Texas Revolution," chapter 9; William C. Davis, *Three Roads to the Alamo: The Lives and Fortunes of David Crockett, James Bowie, and William Barret Travis* (New York: HarperCollins, 1998), 489. General Mexía's defeat at Tampico did not become known until early December. See Mexía to Viesca, Dec. 3, 1835, in Jenkins (ed.), *PTR*, III, 89–90; Mexía to Smith, Dec. 7, 1835, Jenkins (ed.), *PTR*, III, 106–110. Governor Smith, like Houston, then became wary of Mexía, and consequently wrote him off. See Smith to Council, Dec. 9, 1835, Jenkins (ed.), *PTR*, III, 129.

⁸ Reid, *Secret War for Texas*, 62.

⁹ Harbert Davenport, "Men of Goliad," *Southwestern Historical Quarterly* 43 (July 1939): 1–41; Stuart Reid, *The Texan Army 1835–46* (Oxford, UK: Osprey Publishing, 2003).

¹⁰ Reid, *Secret War for Texas*, 54–55.

¹¹ Grant to Austin, Nov. 13, 1835, in Jenkins (ed.), *PTR*, II, 395–96. Frank W. Johnson later admitted in the manuscript version of his *A History of Texas and the Texans* "that such an expedition was spoken of, freely discussed, is true," and he defensively took issue with Yoakum's assertions about Grant. Still, Johnson published Grant's letter to Austin in his book: *A History of Texas and Texans*, ed. Eugene C. Barker and Ernest William Winkler (5 vols.; Chicago: American Historical Society, 1914), I, 363–64. Dudley Goodall Wooten's 1898 reprint of Yoakum's history included commentary from Johnson's then unpublished manuscript. See Wooten (ed.), *A Comprehensive History of Texas, 1685–1897* (2 vols.; 1898; reprint, Austin: Texas State Historical Association, 1986), I, 195–96, 209–11.

¹² Reid, *Secret War for Texas*, 27.

¹³ John J. Linn, *Reminiscences of Fifty Years in Texas* (1883; reprint, Austin: State House Books, 1986), 300–01.

¹⁴ Johnson to Council, Jan. 7, 1836, in Jenkins (ed.), *PTR*, III, 438–41.

¹⁵ Emphasis in the original. Austin to Johnson, et al., Dec. 22, 1835, in Jenkins (ed.), *PTR*, III, 282–83; Austin to Provisional Government, Dec. 22, 1835, Jenkins (ed.), *PTR*, III, 284–86; Huson, *Phillip Dimmitt's Commandancy of Goliad*, 164.

¹⁶ Johnson to Robinson, Dec. 25, 1835, in Charles Adams Gulick Jr., Harriet Smither, et al. (eds.) *The Papers of Mirabeau Buonaparte Lamar* (6 vols.; 1921–27; reprint, Austin: Pemberton Press, 1968), I, 272–73, hereafter cited as Gulick, et al. (eds.), *Lamar Papers*; Johnson to Smith, Dec. 17, 1835, in Jenkins (ed.), *PTR*, III, 227; Johnson to Governor, Dec. 18, 1835, Jenkins (ed.), *PTR*, III, 244–45; Huson, *Dimmitt's Commandancy of Goliad*, 144–45.

¹⁷ Fernando De León and Carlos Laso to Philip Dimmitt, Dec. 18, 1835, quoted in

Thomas Ricks Lindley, *Alamo Traces: New Evidence and New Conclusions* (Plano: Republic of Texas Press, 2003), 324–25.

[18] See Lindley, *Alamo Traces*, 325–27.

[19] Reid, *Secret War for Texas*, 66, 91–93; Statement of Gen. Wm. G. Cooke, Feb. 1844, in Gulick, et al., (eds.), *Lamar Papers*, IV (part 1), 42–43; Neill to Governor & Council, Jan. 6, 1836, in Jenkins (ed.), *PTR*, III, 424–25.

[20] See Johnson to Council, Jan. 3, 1836, in Jenkins (ed.), *PTR*, IV, 412–13.

[21] Reid, *Secret War for Texas*, 79–80.

[22] Henry Millard to [?], Jan. 14, 1836 , as quoted in Yoakum's *History of Texas*, in Wooten (ed.), *Comprehensive History of Texas*, I, 216. For his service in the battle of San Jacinto, Houston presented Lieutenant Colonel Millard with Santa Anna's captured dueling pistols, now in the Republic of Texas Museum, Austin, Texas.

[23] Huson, *Refugio*, I, 264; Huson, *Dimmitt's Commandancy of Goliad*, 227–32.

[24] See Stephen Hardin, *The Alamo 1836: Santa Anna's Texas Campaign* (Westport, Conn.: Praeger, 2004), 52; Lindley, *Alamo Traces*, 297–309; Charles M. Yates, "The 1824 Flag of the Texas Revolution" and "The Alamo Flag," TexianLegacy.com, <http://www.texianlegacy.com/1824_2.html> and <http://www.texianlegacy.com/1824flag.html> [Accessed Aug. 26, 2011].

[25] F. W. Johnson, "Proclamation of the Federal Volunteer Army of Texas," Jan. 10, 1836, in Jenkins (ed.), *PTR*, III, 467–68; Reid, *Secret War for Texas*, 86–87.

[26] Goliad Declaration of Independence, Dec. 20, 1835, in H. P. N. Gamel, comp., *The Laws of Texas* (10 vols.; Austin: Gammel Book Co., 1898), I, 817–20; Huson, *Dimmitt's Commandancy of Goliad*, 69.

[27] John J. Linn to Austin, Nov. 11, 1835, in Jenkins (ed.), *PTR*, II, 379; The Holy Bible [King James Version], Joshua 9: 21, 23, 27 (New York: American Bible Society by D. & G. Bruce, 1827).

[28] Huson, *Dimmitt's Commandancy of Goliad*, 198–220; Lack, *Texas Revolutionary Experience*, 58, 149–50.

[29] Statement of Gen. Wm. G. Cooke, Feb. 1844, Gulick, et al. (eds.), *Lamar Papers*, IV (part 1), 42–43; Bowie to Houston, Jan. 10, 1836, quoted in Davis, *Lone Star Rising*, 191; Huson, *Refugio*, I, 264; Huson, *Dimmitt's Commandancy of Goliad*, 227–32.

Chapter 6

[1] Huson, *Dimmitt's Commandancy of Goliad*, 202, 228n; Reid, *Secret War for Texas*, 69–88; W. Roy Smith, "The Quarrel between Governor Smith and the Council of the Provisional Government of the Republic," *Quarterly of the Texas State Historical Association* 5 (April 1902): 269–346, esp. 296–305, 312–19. See also Lack, *Texas Revolutionary Experience*, xiii–xiv, 54–60, 63; Hardin, *Texian Iliad*, 106–09.

[2] Davis, *Three Roads to the Alamo*, 492; Wharton quoted in Yoakum's *History of Texas*, in Wooten (ed.), *Comprehensive History of Texas*, I, 223.

[3] Johnson's fiery "Proclamation of the Federal Volunteer Army of Texas," reads in part:
The Federal Volunteer army of Texas, the victors of San Antonio, then and now under the command of Francis W. Johnson . . . Under sanction of the general council of Texas . . . have taken up the line of march for the country west of the Rio Grande . . .

To arms! then, Americans, to aid in sustaining the principles of 1776, in this western hemisphere. To arms! native Mexicans, in driving tyranny from your homes, intolerance from your altars, and the tyrant from your country . . . Not only Texas and the Mexicans, but the genius of liberty, demands that every man do his duty, to his country and leave the consequences to God. Our first attack will be upon Matamoros; our next, if Heaven decrees, wherever tyranny shall raise its malignant form.

Johnson, Proclamation of the Federal Volunteer Army of Texas, Jan.10, 1836, in Jenkins (ed.), *PTR*, III, 467–68.

[4] Smith to General Council, Jan. 9, 1836, *Journal of the Proceedings of the General Council of the Republic of Texas held at San Felipe de Austin, November 14th, 1835–March 11th, 1836*, 211–13.

[5] In a public proclamation defending its actions against Smith's accusations, the General Council disclaimed ever having given Grant authority for his actions at San Antonio: "This Council . . . denies having ever recognized in Dr. Grant any authority whatever, as an officer of the Government or army at the time." Council to People of Texas, Jan. 11, 1836, in Jenkins (ed.), *PTR*, III, 470–75. See also Houston to Smith, Jan. 30, 1836, in Barker and Williams (eds.), *Writings of Sam Houston*, I, 344–55.

[6] Smith to Ward, Jan. 6, 1836, in Jenkins (ed.), *PTR*, III, 427–29; Fannin to Robinson, Jan. 21, 1836, Jenkins (ed.), *PTR*, IV, 103–06; Ward to Committee, Feb. 20, 1836, Jenkins (ed.), *PTR*, IV, 388–90; Davenport, "James W. Fannin's Part in the Texas Revolution," chapter 11; Roell, *Remember Goliad!*, 65.

[7] Houston to Smith, Jan. 30, 1836, in Barker and Williams (eds.), *Writings of Sam Houston*, I, 344–55.

[8] Houston to Smith, Jan. 17, 1836, in Barker and Williams (eds.), *Writings of Sam Houston*, I, 339–40. For Bowie's whereabouts and actions between the time of Houston's issuing him the "request" to begin the Matamoros expedition, which he did not receive but learned about later, and his arrival at Goliad immediately preceding Houston's, see Davis, *Three Roads to the Alamo*, 485–94.

[9] Houston to Smith, Jan. 17, 1836, Barker and Williams (eds.), *Writings of Sam Houston*, I, 339–40; Houston to Smith, Jan. 30, 1836, in Barker and Williams (eds.), *Writings of Sam Houston*, I, 344–55.

[10] Hardin, *Texian Iliad*, 110.

[11] For example, Barker and Williams cite Houston's attributed speech as "To the Soldiers at Goliad," Jan. 15 [?], 1836, based on an account by Hermann Ehrenberg; see *Writings of Sam Houston*, I, 337–39. Respected Houston biographer M. K. Wisehart noted, "No complete version of Houston's powerful appeal to the soldiers at Goliad exists. It is one of two important 'lost' speeches, but fragments in various sources agree in essentials." See M. K. Wisehart, *Sam Houston: American Giant* (Washington, D.C.: Robert B. Luce, 1963), 150–53, 658n7. This mistake is repeated elsewhere.

[12] James E. Crisp, "Sam Houston's Speechwriters: The Grad Student, the Teenager, the Editors, and the Historians," *Southwestern Historical Quarterly* 97 (October 1993): 203–37.

[13] Houston to Smith, Jan. 17, 1836, Barker and Williams (eds.), *Writings of Sam Houston*, I, 339–40; Houston to Smith, Jan. 30, 1836, in Barker and Williams (eds.), *Writings of Sam Houston*, I, 344–55.

[14] Houston asserted that the powers given to Fannin as agent of the council "are as comprehensive in their nature, and as much at variance with the organic law . . . as the decrees of the general Congress of Mexico are at variance with the federal constitution of 1824, and really delegate to J. W. Fannin, jr., as extensive powers as those conferred by the Congress on General Santa Anna." Houston to Smith, Jan. 30, 1836, in Barker and Williams (eds.), *Writings of Sam Houston*, I, 344–55.

[15] Houston to Smith, Jan. 17, 1836, in Barker and Williams (eds.), *Writings of Sam Houston*, I, 339–40.

[16] Houston to Smith, Jan. 30, 1836, in Barker and Williams (eds.), *Writings of Sam Houston*, I, 344–55.

[17] The traditional source of Houston's speech is Hermann Ehrenberg, *With Milam and Fannin: Adventures of a German Boy in Texas' Revolution*, trans. Charlotte Churchill (Austin: Pemberton Press, 1968), 129–30. See also Crisp, "Sam Houston's Speechwriters"; and James E. Crisp, "In Pursuit of Herman Ehrenberg: A Research Adventure," *Southwestern Historical Quarterly* 102 (April 1999), 423–40.

[18] Account of Reuben R. Brown, in Gulick, et al. (eds.), *Lamar Papers*, V, 367–72; Ehrenberg, *With Milam and Fannin*, 129; Hardin, *Texian Iliad*, 110; Reid, *Secret War for Texas*, 103–04, 107.

[19] Houston to Smith, Jan. 30, 1836, in Barker and Williams (eds.), *Writings of Sam Houton*, I, 344–55; Smith to Houston, Jan. 28, 1836, in Jenkins (ed.), *PTR*, IV, 176; Davenport, "James W. Fannin's Part in the Texas Revolution," chapter 12; Randolph B. Campbell, *Sam Houston and the American Southwest* (New York: HarperCollins, 1993), 56–57; Hardin, *Texian Iliad*, 110–11; Wisehart, *Sam Houston*, 157–58. Houston's own account, as told to Charles Edwards Lester, is useful if used with caution. See *Life of General Sam Houston: A Short Autobiography* (1852 [?]; reprint, Austin: Pemberton Press, 1964). For Johnson's version, see Johnson to Council, Jan. 30. 1836, in Jenkins (ed.), *PTR*, IV, 197–99.

[20] Proceedings of a Citizens' and Soldiers' Meeting at Béxar relative to the General Council & Gov. H. Smith, etc., Jan. 26, 1836, in Gulick, et al. (eds.), *Lamar Papers*, V, 93–94. Historian William C. Davis calls this "Béxar's declaration of independence from the false authorities that ignored and abused the garrison" and "the irrevocable announcement of Bowie and the rest that so long as this internal discord plagued the provisional government and the rest of its forces, they intended to stay there, come what may." Davis, *Three Roads to the Alamo*, 499.

[21] Fannin to Robinson, Feb. 4, 1836, which contains excerpts from Johnson to Fannin, Feb. 2, 1836, in Gulick, et al. (eds.), *Lamar Papers*, I, 315–16.

[22] Ibid.

[23] Ibid; Linn, *Reminiscences*, 124.

[24] Fannin to Robinson, Feb. 4, 1836; Reuben Brown quoted in Johnson, *Texas and Texans*, I, 422.

Chapter 7

[1] José de Urrea, Diario, Jan. 15–31, 1836, in Carlos E. Castañeda (ed.), *Mexican Side of the Texas Revolution* (2nd ed.; Austin: Graphic Ideas, 1970), 217–19; De la Peña, *With Santa Anna in Texas*, 67.

[2] Fisher's remarks in James Power's report to the General Council, Dec. 17, 1835, in *Journal of the Proceedings of the General Council of the Republic of Texas held at San Felipe de Austin, November 14th, 1835–March 11th, 1836*, 126; Johnson to Robinson, Feb. 9, 1836, in Gulick, et al. (eds.), *Lamar Papers*, I, 322–23.

[3] Edwin R. Sweeney, *Mangas Coloradas, Chief of the Chiricahua Apaches* (Norman: University of Oklahoma Press, 1998), 81.

[4] David G. Burnet, Proclamation to the People of Texas, June 20, 1836, quoted in De Witt Clinton Baker, *A Texas Scrap-book: Made Up of the History, Biography, and Miscellany of Texas and Its People* (New York: A. S. Barnes & Co., 1875), 332; Proclamation of the State Government of Sonora, 1838, quoted in F. T. Dávila, *Sonora histórico y descriptivo* (Nogales, Ariz.: Tipografía de R. Bernal, 1894), 21.

[5] José María Tornel y Mendívil, *Tejas y los Estados-Unidos de América en sus relaciones con la república Mexicana* (1837), trans. in Castañeda (ed.), *Mexican Side of the Texas Revolution*, 362; Santa Anna, *Manifesto*, in Castañeda (ed.), *Mexican Side of the Texas Revolution*, 16.

[6] Donald T. Garate, *Juan Bautista De Anza: Basque Explorer in the New World* (Reno: University of Nevada Press, 2005), 158–59; Stephen T. Bass, "Basques in the Americas from 1492 to 1850: A Chronology," (September 2008), <http://www.nabasque.org/pdf/Basque_Chronology_February_2008.pdf> [Accessed Aug. 26, 2011; Gerardo Palomo González, "La inestilidad politico-militar durante la primera república central, 1835–1839: La lógica del pro-

nunciamiento en la figura del general José Urrea," *Estudios de historia moderna y contemporánea de México* 36 (July–December 2008): 99–100; Henry F. Dobyns, *Spanish Colonial Tucson: A Demographic History* (Tucson: University of Arizona Press, 1976), 107–08, 204–205n18; Francisco R. Almada, *Diccionario de historia, geografía, y biografía sonorenses* (Chihuahua, Chihuahua: Ruiz Sandoval, 1952), 806–10; Patricia Roche Herring, "Tucsonense Preclaro (Illustrious Tucsonan), General José C. Urrea, Romantic Idealist," *Journal of Arizona History* 34 (Autumn 1993): 307–20. See also Patricia Roche Herring, *General José Cosme Urrea: His Life and Times, 1797–1849* (Spokane, Wash.: Arthur H. Clark, 1995).

[7] Urrea, Diario, Jan. 22–31, 1836, in Castañeda (ed.), *Mexican Side of the Texas Revolution*, 218–19; Morris to Fannin, Feb. 6, 1836, in Jenkins (ed.), *PTR*, IV, 274–76.

[8] Urrea, Diario, Jan. 21–31, 1836, in Castañeda (ed.), *Mexican Side of the Texas Revolution*, 218–19; De la Peña, *With Santa Anna in Texas,* 67–68.

[9] De la Peña, *With Santa Anna in Texas*, 68; Gobierno del Departmento Tamaulipas, Circular, José Antonio Fernández, Dec. 8, 1835; Urrea, Diario, Jan. 22–1836, in Castañeda (ed.), *Mexican Side of the Texas Revolution*, 218–19.

[10] Lack, *Texas Revolutionary Experience*, 160–64; Urrea, Diario, Jan 21–Feb. 19, 1836, in Castañeda (ed.), *Mexican Side of the Texas Revolution*, 218–19; Taylor, "Dr. Grant and His Matamoros Expedition Starts Trouble," <http://www.tamu.edu/ccbn/dewitt/goliadcreed.htm> [Accessed Aug. 26, 2011]. See also Alonzo Salazar, "Don Carlos de la Garza, Loyalist Leader," in De la Teja (ed.), *Tejano Leadership in Mexican and Revolutionary Texas,* 194–211; and Hardin, "Efficient in the Cause," in *Tejano Journey,* 64. On Urrea's troop strength, see Reid, *Secret War for Texas*, 134 and 215n11. Estimate of Tejano rancheros is from Roy Grimes, *Goliad: 130 Years After* (Victoria, Tex.: Victoria Advocate Printing Co., 1966).

[11] Benavides quoted in Morris to Fannin, Feb. 6, 1836, in Jenkins (ed.), *PTR*, IV, 274–76; Statement of Gen. Wm. G. Cooke (regarding Morris), Feb. 1844, in Gulick, et al. (eds.), *Lamar Papers*, IV (part 1), 42–43. See also Davenport, "James W. Fannin's Part in the Texas Revolution," chapters 13 and 14, and Reid, *Secret War for Texas*, 122–24.

[12] Antonio Menchaca, "Memoirs," in *The Alamo Remembered: Tejano Accounts and Perspectives,* ed. Timothy M. Matovina (Austin: University of Texas Press, 1995), 118–19; Creed Taylor, "Dr. Grant and His Matamoros Expedition Starts Trouble," <http://www.tamu.edu/ccbn/dewitt/goliadcreed.htm> [Accessed Aug. 26, 2011].

[13] Johnson to Fannin, Feb. 9, 1836, in Gulick, et al. (eds.), *Lamar Papers*, I, 321–22; Austin's comment found in Austin to George Fisher, Jan. 15, 1834, Texas State Library and Archives Commission, <http://www.tsl.state.tx.us/treasures/giants/austin/austin-fisher-jan34-1.html> [Accessed Aug. 26, 2011]; Reid, *Secret War for Texas*, 126.

[14] Johnson to Fannin, Feb. 9, 1836, in Gulick, et al. (eds.), *Lamar Papers*, I, 321–22.

[15] Roberts and Olson, *Line in the Sand*, 76; Reid, *Secret War for Texas*, 128; De la Peña, *With Santa Anna in Texas*, 18–19; Fannin's strategy is noted in a letter by his adjutant, John Sowers Brooks, to Mary Ann Brooks, Feb. 25, 1836, in Jenkins (ed.), *PTR*, IV, 424–26.

[16] Robinson to Fannin, Feb. 13, 1836, Gulick, et al. (eds.), *Lamar Papers*, I, 330; Robinson to Fannin, Feb. 13, 1836 (separate letter from the preceding one), Gulick, et al. (eds.), *Lamar Papers*, I, 330–31; "Advisory Committee" to Robinson, Feb. 15, 1836, in Jenkins (ed.), *PTR*, IV, 340–41; Davenport, "James W. Fannin's Part in the Texas Revolution," chapter 19.

[17] Robinson's order quoted in Yoakum's *History of Texas*, in Wooten (ed.), *Comprehensive History of Texas,* I, 249.

[18] Lack, *Texas Revolutionary Experience,* 163; Garay quoted in Vicente Filísola, *Memorias para la historia de la guerra de Tejas*, segunda parte (México, D.F.: Tipografía de R. Rafael, 1849), II, 405.

[19] Statement of Gen. Wm. G. Cooke (regarding Morris), Feb. 1844, in Gulick, et al. (eds.), *Lamar Papers*, IV (part 1), 42–43; Davenport, "James W. Fannin's Part in the Texas Revolution," chapter 14.

[20] Reid, *Secret War for Texas*, 129–33; Urrea, Diario, Jan. 22–31, 1836, in Castañeda (ed.), *Mexican Side of the Texas Revolution*, 218–19.

[21] Fannin's intelligence even named the correct Mexican commanders en route: "Scizma" (Joaquín Ramírez y Sesma), "Felisola" (Vicente Filisola) and "Cos" (Martín Perfecto de Cos) to San Antonio; "Uria" (José de Urrea) and "Garay" (Francisco Garay) to Goliad; and the division under Santa Anna himself. Fannin to Robinson, Feb. 16, 1836, in Gulick, et al. (eds.), *Lamar Papers*, I, 332–34. On the Goliad Campaign of 1836, see Roell, *Remember Goliad!*, 45–73.

[22] Fannin to Robinson, Feb. 14, 1836, quoted in *Texas and the Texans*, by Henry Stuart Foote (2 vols., 1841; reprint, Austin: The Steck Co., 1935), II, 206; Fannin to Robinson, Feb. 22, 1836, in Jenkins (ed.), *PTR*, IV, 398–401 (emphasis in original); Fannin to Joseph Mims, Feb. 28, 1836, Jenkins (ed.), *PTR*, IV, 454; Fannin to Robinson, Mar. 1, 1836, included with the letter of Feb. 22, previously cited, also quoted in Wooten (ed.), *Comprehensive History of Texas*, I, 248n–49n. See also Fannin to Robinson, Feb. 7, 1836, in Jenkins (ed.), *PTR*, IV, 279–81; and Fannin to Robinson, Feb. 17, 1836, Jenkins (ed.), *PTR*, IV, 371.

[23] McMullen-McGloin Account of the Johnson-Grant Expedition, from *The Papers of Mirabeau Lamar*, No. 1658, Sons of DeWitt Colony Texas, <http://www.tamu.edu/faculty/ccbn/dewitt/goliadsanpat.htm> [Accessed Aug. 26, 2011]; Roell, *Remember Goliad!*, chapters 3 and 4; Reid, *Secret War for Texas*, 131–34.

[24] Urrea, Diario, Feb. 26–27, 1836, in Castañeda (ed.), *Mexican Side of the Texas Revolution*, 220–23; De la Peña, *With Santa Anna in Texas*, 68–69; Roell, *Remember Goliad!*, chapters 3 and 4; Reid, *Secret War for Texas*, 133–38.

[25] Urrea, Diario, Feb. 26–27, 1836, in Castañeda (ed.), *Mexican Side of the Texas Revolution*, 220–23; De la Peña, *With Santa Anna in Texas*, 68–69; Rodríguez to José M. Guerra, Mar. 7, 1836, in Jenkins (ed.), *PTR*, V, 20; Reid, *Secret War for Texas*, 140–44, 215n22; Ana Carolina Castillo Crimm, "Finding Their Way," in Gerald Eugene Poyo, *Tejano Journey, 1770–1850* (Austin: University of Texas Press, 1996), 119; Hardin, "Benavides," 65–66.

[26] Account of Reuben R. Brown in Gulick, et al. (eds.), *Lamar Papers*, V, 367–72; on Brown's various accounts, see also Reid, *Secret War for Texas*, 144–46; Brown's statement about Grant being well known, see Brown's account in Wooten (ed.), *Comprehensive History of Texas*, I, 244–46; De la Peña, *With Santa Anna in Texas*, 69.

[27] Brown's account in Gulick, et al. (eds.), *Lamar Papers*, V, 370. On Benavides and the De Leóns, see Roell, *Remember Goliad!*, 50, 66, 68, 73, 74–75; Roell, "Benavides, Plácido," *The New Handbook of Texas*, I, 484; Roell, "De León, Fernando," *The New Handbook of Texas*, II, 570 –71; and Roell, "De León's Colony," *The New Handbook of Texas*, II, 574-74.

[28] Johnson, *A History of Texas and Texans*, I, 382–85.

[29] De la Peña, *With Santa Anna in Texas*, 144.

[30] See Roell, *Remember Goliad!*, 45–73. Recent traditional military histories specifically examining Fannin at Goliad include Jay A. Stout, *Slaughter at Goliad: The Mexican Massacre of 400 Texas Volunteers* (Annapolis, Md.: U.S. Naval Institute Press, 2008); William R. Bradle, *Goliad: The Other Alamo* (Gretna, La.: Pelican Publishing, 2007); Gary Brown, *Hesitant Martyr in the Texas Revolution: James Walker Fannin* (Dallas: Republic of Texas Press, 2000); and Clifford Hopewell, *Remember Goliad: Their Silent Tents* (Austin: Eakin Press, 1998).

[31] Fannin to Robinson, Feb. 22, 1836, in Jenkins (ed.), *PTR*, IV, 398–401; Fannin to Robinson, Feb. 26, 1836, Jenkins (ed.), *PTR*, IV, 443–44; Fannin to Robinson, Feb. 28, 1836, Jenkins (ed.), *PTR*, IV, 455–56; Dr. Joseph H. Barnard, *Dr. Joseph H. Barnard's Journal: A Composite of Known Versions of the Journal of Dr. Joseph H. Barnard*, ed. Hobart Huson (Refugio, Tex. [?]: n.p., 1949), 14; Urrea, Diario, Feb. 27, 1836, in Castañeda (ed.), *Mexican Side of the Texas Revolution*, 222–23.

[32] Fannin to Capts. Francis Desauque and Chenworth [Chenoweth], Mar. 1, 1836, in

Jenkins (ed.), *PTR*, IV, 477–78; Hardin, *Texian Iliad*, 135, 160–61; Roell, *Remember Goliad!*, 48, 50, 52.

[33] John Sowers Brooks to his mother, Mar. 2, 1836, in Jenkins (ed.), *PTR*, IV, 485–88; Burr H. Duval to William P. Duval, Mar. 9, 1836, Jenkins (ed.), *PTR*, V, 33–35; J. G. Ferguson to A. J. Ferguson, Mar. 2, 1836, Jenkins (ed.), *PTR*, IV, 488–89.

[34] Fannin to Robinson, Feb. 7, 1836, in Jenkins (ed.), *PTR*, IV, 279–81; *The Holy Bible* [King James Version], 1 Kings 18:21.

[35] Fannin to Robinson, Feb. 22, 1836, in Jenkins (ed.), *PTR*, IV, 398–401 (emphasis in the oirginal); Robinson to Fannin, Mar. 6, 1836, Jenkins (ed.), *PTR*, V, 10–11.

[36] Fannin to Mexía, Mar. 11, 1836, in Jenkins (ed.), *PTR*, V, 47–48.

[37] Houston to Fannin, Mar. 11, 1836, in Jenkins (ed.), *PTR*, V, 51; Houston to Fannin, Mar. 11, 1836 (separate letter), Jenkins (ed.), *PTR*, V, 52–53; Roell, *Remember Goliad!*, 52–60.

[38] Houston to James Collinsworth, Mar. 13, 1836, in Barker and Williams (eds.), *Writings of Sam Houston*, I, 367–68 (emphasis in the original). Houston's phrase reads, "I would [rather than could] not rely on any co-operation from him," as printed in Jenkins (ed.), *PTR*, V, 64–71. The phrase as printed in Yoakum's *History of Texas* (p. 474) is "could not."

[39] Roell, *Remember Goliad!*, 56–73. See also Craig H. Roell, "Coleto, Battle of," *The New Handbook of Texas*, II, 205–07; Roell," "Refugio, Battle of," *The New Handbook of Texas*, V, 512; and Harbert Davenport and Craig H. Roell, "Goliad Massacre," III, 218–21. Historian Will Fowler emphasizes that both Urrea and Portilla "were traumatized by the experience of implementing this order." See Fowler, *Santa Anna of Mexico*, 169. The battle of Coleto is memorialized as Fannin Battleground State Historic Site, although ironically, the surrounding live oak woods that designate the Mexican name for the battlefield now host a gated lake front community called Perdido Pointe Estates.

[40] Fowler, *Santa Anna of Mexico*, 175–78.

[41] Vicente Filísola, *Memorias para la historia de la guerra de Tejas* (2 vols.; México, D.F.: Impr. de I. Cumplido, 1849), I, 239; De la Peña, *With Santa Anna in Texas*, 158–59, 166; Urrea, *Diario*, Apr. 26–30, 1836, in Castañeda (ed.), *Mexican Side of the Texas Revolution*, 256–62; Gregg J. Dimmick, *Sea of Mud: The Retreat of the Mexican Army after San Jacinto, An Archeological Investigation* (Austin: Texas State Historical Association, 2006), 290.

Chapter 8

[1] Jovita González and Eve Raleigh, *Caballero: A Historical Novel*, eds. José E. Limón and María Cotera (College Station: Texas A&M University Press, 1996), 161. Written in the 1930s and 1940s and published posthumously, few books have captured so poignantly the heartrending difficulties and complexity of life for Mexicans in South Texas in the aftermath of the Texas Revolution and the U.S.-Mexican War. Jovita González de Mireles (1904–83) was a respected folklorist and historian of Mexican culture, particularly of the Rio Grande Valley, and a protégé of historian Eugene C. Barker and folklorist J. Frank Dobie.

[2] See Dimmick, *Sea of Mud*, and Vicente Filisola, *General Vicente Filisola's Analysis of José Urrea's Military Diary: A Forgotten 1838 Publication by an Eyewitness to the Texas Revolution*, ed. Gregg J. Dimmick and trans. John R. Wheat (Austin: Texas State Historical Association, 2007); Fowler, *Santa Anna of Mexico*, 177.

[3] Zárate-Ruiz, *Matamoros*, 41 (quotation). The standard works are Donaly E. Brice, *The Great Comanche Raid: Boldest Indian Attack of the Texas Republic* (Austin: Eakin Press, 1987); and Joseph Milton Nance, *After San Jacinto: The Texas-Mexican Frontier, 1836–1841* (Austin: University of Texas Press, 1963). These should now be supplemented with Stephen L. Moore, *Savage Frontier: Rangers, Riflemen, and Indian Wars in Texas, Volume III, 1840–41* and *Volume IV, 1842–45* (Denton: University of North Texas Press, 2007, 2010). See also Octavio Herrera Pérez, *El norte de Tamaulipas y la conformación de la frontera México-Estados Unidos, 1835–1855*

(Ciudad Victoria: El Colegio de Tamaulipas, 2003).

[4] Zárate-Ruiz, *Matamoros*, 49. The Spanish reads, "Sólo anexándose a los Estados Unidos, los texanos podrían llevar adelante su pretensión de extender los límites de su territorio hasta el Bravo." See also Rosaura Alicia Dávila y Oscar Rivera Saldaña, *Matamoros en la guerra con los Estados Unidos* (Matamoros, Tamaulipas: Ediciones Archivo Histórico-Sociedad de Historia, 1996).

[5] Jerry D. Thompson, *Cortina: Defending the Mexican Name in Texas* (College Station: Texas A&M University Press, 2007), 11; Hamalainen, *Comanche Empire*, 229.

[6] Valerio-Jiménez, "Neglected Citizens and Willing Traders," 294–95; Robert A. Potash, *Mexican Government and Industrial Development in the Early Republic: The Banco de Avío* (Amherst: University of Massachusetts Press, 1983), 131.

[7] Joseph E. Chance, *José María de Jesús Carvajal: The Life and Times of a Mexican Revolutionary* (San Antonio: Trinity University Press, 2006), esp. 9–10, 51–55, 61–73; Josefina Zoraida Vázquez, "La supuesta República del Río Grande" ["The supposed Republic of the Rio Grande"], in *Historia Mexicana* 36 (July–September, 1986), <http://www.crwflags.com/fotw/flags/mx-rgr.html> [Accessed Aug. 26, 2011]. By contrast, Leslie Alice Jones Wagner asserts evidence that the republic did indeed exist; see "Disputed Territory: Río Grande/Río Bravo Borderlands, 1838–1840" (MA thesis, University of Texas at Arlington, 1998). Miguel A. González Quiroga and César Morado Macías refer to the charismatic Canales as "*el camaleónico*," the chameleon. See *Nuevo León ocupado: aspectos de la guerra* México-*Estados Unidos* (Monterrey: Fondo Editorial de Nuevo León, 2006), 148.

[8] Gen. Francísco Mejía, Proclamation, Mar. 18, 1846, in Steven R. Butler (ed.), *A Documentary History of the Mexican War* (Richardson, Tex.: Descendants of Mexican War Veterans, 1995), 25; Joseph Wheelan, *Invading Mexico: America's Continental Dream and the Mexican War, 1846–1848* (New York: Carroll & Graf, 2007), 85.

[9] Zárate-Ruiz, *Matamoros*, 57.

[10] Denise Spellberg, "Inventing Matamoros: Gender and the Forgotten Islamic Past in the United States of America," *Frontiers: A Journal of Women Studies* 25, No. 1 (2004), 156, 150 (cited in order of quotations); Robert Walter Johannsen, *To the Halls of the Montezumas: The Mexican War in the American Imagination* (New York: Oxford University Press, 1985), 11–12, 219, 233. See also Michael Scott Van Wagenen, *Remembering the Forgotten War: The Enduring Legacies of the U.S-Mexican War* (Amherst: University of Massachusetts Press, 2012), a superb history that details how the U.S.-Mexican War influences the complex relationship between Mexico and the United States to this day. Regarding Matamoros, the book's treatment of the transnational considerations in creating Palo Alto Battlefield National Historical Park is especially noteworthy.

[11] Chance, *José María de Jesús Carvajal*, esp. 5, 10, 82–102, 145–46; Eliseo Paredes Manzano, *Conmemoración del CXXXI Aniversario de los Honrosos Títulos de Heróica, Leal e Invicta* (Matamoros, Tamaulipas: R. Ayuntaminto 1981–83, 1982), 10, 12, quoted in Zárate-Ruiz, *Matamoros*, 62–64. Andrés Reséndez puts the two unsuccessful attempts to establish a separate federalist republic of the Rio Grande into the larger perspective of numerous secessionist movements that occurred in Texas, Tamaulipas, New Mexico, Alta and Baja California, Tabasco, and Yucatán, which "bespeak of bitter and protracted power struggles" between federalists and centralists. See Reséndez, *Changing National Identities at the Frontier*, 265–67.

[12] Warner P. Sutton, "Commerce and Trade of Mexico," in *Reports of the Consuls of the United States*, vol. 29 (Washington, D.C.: U.S. Government Printing Office, 1888), 711.

[13] <http://charrodaysfiesta.com> [Accessed Aug. 26, 2012].

[14] Ramón Eduardo Ruiz, *On the Rim of Mexico: Encounters of the Rich and Poor* (Boulder, Colo.: Westview Press, 1998), 226.

ACKNOWLEDGMENTS

THERE IS A SENTIMENT that nothing in Texas is without controversy. Certainly this is true about Matamoros and the Texas Revolution.
As in any great family argument, points of view abound; it is with dis-
quietude that one even enters into the discussion. Still, I am thankful for
the opportunity. My own vision was shaped initially by growing up in
Victoria, Texas, just up the road from Goliad, in the heart of this venerable history. Many years later, as a Nelda C. and H. J. Lutcher Stark Foundation Fellow in Texas Studies at the Texas State Historical Association
(TSHA), I wrote about the Matamoros expedition, among other subjects,
for *The New Handbook of Texas* (1996). Ron Tyler, then director of TSHA,
encouraged me to expand my *Handbook* article "Matamoros Expedition
of 1835–36" into a book-length study. I explored the possibilities in a pre-
sentation at the 1998 Symposium on the Early History of the Goliad and
Victoria Area and in a paper prepared for the 2002 TSHA annual meeting.

Janice Pinney, formerly TSHA's interim director of publications, supported my endeavor in its earliest stages. Ryan Schumacher, current associate editor at TSHA, and Randolph "Mike" Campbell, TSHA's chief historian, fostered my manuscript into print. I am indebted to them and to
Bonnie Lovell for her advice and thorough critique of the manuscript,
which have made for a much better book. I appreciate the special map
created by Alexander Mendoza at the University of North Texas, and the
labor of book designer David Timmons and indexer Cindy Coan. I am
grateful to the many scholars identified in the notes. To name one would
require naming them all; simply put, their excellent works informed this
book and made it possible. Beyond their superb scholarship, James E.
Crisp, Stephen L. Hardin, Jesús "Frank" de la Teja, and Stuart Reid per-
sonally encouraged my own efforts. Moreover, I am grateful to the wealth
of resources made available by the city of Heróica Matamoros, Tamaulipas, Mexico; the Colegio de la Frontero Norte (El Colef); the University of Texas at Brownsville and Texas Southmost College; the Nettie Lee
Benson Latin American Collection and the Dolph Briscoe Center for

American History at my doctoral alma mater, the University of Texas at Austin; the websites of the Sons of DeWitt Colony Texas and of Alamo de Parras, both part of The Texian Web; the Texas State Library and Archives Commission; the Texas State Historical Association, notably *The Handbook of Texas Online* and the archive of the *Southwestern Historical Quarterly*; the University of North Texas Portal to Texas History; the Presidio La Bahía, Goliad, Texas; the Tejano Association for Historic Preservation; the Society of Hispanic Historical and Ancestral Research (SomosPrimos.com); and Google Books. I acquired vintage illustrations through US and UK sellers on eBay.com. Special thanks to Samantha Dodd and the Dallas Historical Society, Maps of the Past, Inc., and to Tom McDonald of Fort Worth, Texas, who allowed me to read parts of the biography he is writing of Goliad Massacre survivor James Hughes Callahan, which contains an unsurpassed analysis of William Ward's Georgia Battalion and the battle of Refugio.

At Georgia Southern University, I am grateful to the former chair of the history department, Sandra J. Peacock, for helping me to acquire academic leave allowing time to research this project; to my colleague and social historian of Mexico Laura Shelton for critiquing the manuscript; to my colleagues James M. Woods, Emerson "Tom" McMullen, Michael Scott Van Wagenen, and Johnathan O'Neill for their indefatigable support; to the interlibrary loan staff at Henderson Library; and to Eagle Print Shop, especially Hal Cartee, for help with illustrations. My mother, Ruth M. Roell, provided me the wisdom of her ninety-one years, immeasurable encouragement, and pertinent articles from the *Victoria Advocate*. I owe incomparable gratitude to my wife, Melinda Roell, developmental director and a professional editor and artistic designer for the Averitt Center for the Arts (Statesboro, Georgia), who critiqued the manuscript and helped prepare the illustrations. She stayed sane, wise, and devoted throughout the arduous process. It is to her, and our daughters, that this book is most gratefully dedicated. *Soli Deo gloria.*

About the Author

CRAIG H. ROELL is a native of Victoria, Texas, the son of Henry R. and Ruth M. Roell. He earned his MA and PhD in history from the University of Texas at Austin and was Samuel Davis Postdoctoral Fellow in Business History at Ohio State University. Dr. Roell was a Nelda C. and H. J. Lutcher Stark Foundation Fellow in Texas Studies for the Texas State Historical Association's *New Handbook of Texas* project and was the major contributor to TSHA's *The Handbook of Victoria County* (1990). His book *Remember Goliad! A History of La Bahía* (TSHA, 1994) garnered a La Bahía Award from the Sons of the Republic of Texas, honored as the "Best Shorter Work in Texas History of the Year 1995—Outstanding Contribution in the Field of Spanish Colonial Period." The University of North Carolina Press reissued his earlier book *The Piano in America, 1890–1940* (1989), in its Enduring Editions series in 2009. He has contributed articles to *The Piano: An Encyclopedia* (2003), the *Encyclopedia of Chicago* (2004), the *Encyclopedia of Leadership* (2004), and the *Encyclopedia of Recreation and Leisure in America* (2004). Dr. Roell is Professor of Economic, Business, and Cultural History at Georgia Southern University in Statesboro, where he was named Wells/Warren Professor of the Year (2002, 2013), and is profiled in *Who's Who in America, 2011* (2010). He is married to Melinda H. Roell; they have two daughters, soon two sons-in-law, and too many cats.

INDEX

Page numbers in italics indicate illustrations.

A

African Americans, 35
Agua Dulce Creek, battle of, 4, 17, 78–79,
    80–81
Alamo, battle of
    aftermath of, 82
    Alamo destruction ordered, 61
    correspondence dating to, 83
    defeat, factors in, 80–81
    defenses, state of, 53, 61
    fall of Alamo, word of, 84
    flag flown in, 55
    independence as cause of, 55
    Matamoros compared to, 17
    myths concerning, 6
    overview, 4
    remembering, 6
    stand taken at, 62
Aldrete, José Miguel, 55
Almonte, Juan Nepomuceno, 35
American capitalism, 37, 93
American Civil War, 91
Americans
    filibusters, 6, 7, 40, 68, 74, 80, 90
    imprisonment and execution of, 53
    ships involved in smuggling trade, 33
    trade, Mexican dependence on, 88
    volunteers, 4, 7, 40, 42, 49–50, 52–55,
        59, 60, 61–64, 66, 67–70, 76–78,
        83, 85
Anglo Americans
    in Matamoros, 88–89
    Mexicans, attitudes toward, 16, 42, 52,
        56, 71
    population numbers, 15–16, 42
    rebels, 71
    slavery practiced by, 33, 35

as Texas independence supporters, 55
Anglo Consultation, 42–43
Anglo-Mexican intermarriage, 6
Anglo nation-building, collective memory
    of, 6
Anza, Juan Bautista de, 69
Apache Indians, 35, 41, 42, 88
architecture, 25, 91
Arista, Mariano, 89
Arredondo, Joaquin de, 30
Austin, Stephen F.
    colony established by, 15
    Dimmitt, P., relations with, 46
    Grant, J. correspondence with, 50
    Lemus, P., opinion of, 73
    Linn, J. correspondence with, 56
    Matamoros expedition, attitude
        concerning, 3, 38, 44, 52
    relatives of, 89
    war with Mexico, attitude concerning,
        47
Ávalos, Francisco, 90

B

Bagdad, 18, 23, 29
Barradas, Isidro, 70
Barranco Blanco ranch, 30
Beales, John Charles, 51
Benavides, Plácido
    intelligence gathered by, 72, 73, 74,
        77, 80
    Matamoros expedition, participation in,
        16, 49, 54, 67, 73, 76, 77, 78, 79
    relatives of, 49, 89
    Texas revolution, attitude concerning,
        72
Berlandier, Jean Louis

Comanche warfare noted by, 41
Matamoros described by, 14
road from Matamoros to Goliad
    described by, 22–23
status compared to other foreigners, 31,
    100n13
Béxar
    defense of, 66, 74, 75
    Mexican soldiers on march to, 61, 77
    resolutions, 65–66
    siege of, 3, 49–50, 55, 62, 64
blockades, 88, 91
Bowie, James
    at Alamo, 62
    Alamo destruction, orders received
        by, 61
    Matamoros expedition aid sought from,
        48–49
    Matamoros expedition command
        assumed by, 56–57, 59–60
    Santa Anna, A. L. de, intelligence
        concerning, 72–73
Bradburn, John (Juan) Davis, 31
Brazos Santiago, port at, 53
bridging of cultures, 91–92, 93
Brown, John Henry, 3–4
Brown, Reuben, 64, 67, 79
Brownsville, 90, 91, *91,* 92
Brownsville & Matamoros (B&M)
    International Bridge, *91*
buildings and architecture, 25, 91
Burnet, David G., 69
Bustamante, Anastasio, 13, 40

C

Caballero: A Historical Novel (González and
    Raleigh), 87, 109n1
Calleja, Felix María, 30
Camargo, 12, 76
Cameron, John, 45
Canales Rosillo, Antonio, 66, 67, 76, 89
Capistrán, Macedonio, 90
Carbajal, José María Jesús, 53, 56, 72, 89, 90
Carbajal, Mariano, 55–56
Cárdenas, Jesús de, 89
Chance, Joseph E., 90
chaparral, 19–20, 23
Charro Days Parade, *92*
Cherokee Indians, attempts to recruit, 64
city names, heroes as inspiration for, 10–11

ciudadanos, rights and legal status of, 31
climate, 25–26
Coleto, battle of (Encinal del Perdido), 4,
    72, 77, *81,* 84. *See also* Goliad
Collinsworth, James, 84
colonization laws, U.S. immigration
    restrictions attempted through, 15,
    97n29
Comanche Indians
    attacks and warfare, 2, 13, 87–88
    capture by, risk of, 35
    defense against, 9, 27
    migrations to escape, 29
    tactics of, 73
    Texas domain expanded by, 41–42
Confederacy, 91
Constitution of 1824
    Anglo attitudes concerning, 42, 50, 52,
        55, 56, 58, 66, 68, 87
    attempt to restore, 45, 55
    Matamoros expedition and, 61
    Mexican loyalty to, 70, 72
    rewriting of, 38
    support of, 16
    Texas colonization and, 15
Cooke, William G.
    Fannin, J. W., communication with, 76
    Houston, S., writings concerning, 64
    Matamoros expedition, role in, 49
    reinforcements sent under, 74
    as San Antonio Greys commander, 56
Copano port, 48
Cos, Martín Perfecto de
    arrests made by, 45
    assault against, 44, 48
    Comanche Indians, relations with, 42
    defeat of, 3, 49, 50
    defectors from, 54
    intelligence concerning, 77, 108n21
    at Matamoros headquarters, 33
cotton, 91–92
Crisp, James E., 62
Crockett, David, 72
Cuéllar, Jesús "Comanche," 76
Cuéllar, Salvador, 78
customs house (Matamoros), 9, 25, 32
cyclones and hurricanes, 2, 3, 38

D
Davenport, Harbert, 47

Davis, Graham, 15
Davis, William C., 60
de la Garza, Carlos, 56, 78
de la Garza, Julián, 78
de la Peña, José Enrique
  Grant, J. killing recalled by, 79, 80
  historian's mission, difficulty of fulfilling
    cited by, 6
  marching conditions described by, 86
  Urrea, J. de recalled by, 71, 79, 81
De León, Fernando, 53, 55, 72
De León, Martín, 16
Dewees, William B., 21–22
Diaz Noriega, José María, 35
Dimmick, Gregg J., 85–86, 87
Dimmitt, Philip
  command resigned by, 56, 61
  Grant, J. relations with, 54–55, 56
  Matamoros expedition, attitude
    concerning, 43, 44–45, 52, 55
  Matamoros occupation advocated by,
    47
  Mexicans, attitude toward, 56
  movements of, 83
  as Texas independence supporter, 53,
    55, 66, 72
  Viesca, J. M. opposition to, 46
Dobyns, Henry F., 70
Dolores, colony at, 51
Don Quixote, 10–11
drug smuggling, 93
Duval, Burr H., 76
Duval, John C., 22

E
ebony tree, 20–21
Ehrenberg, Hermann, 63, 64
Encinal del Perdido, 4, 72, 77, 84. See also
  Goliad
Escandón, José de, 12
Escandón, Manuel de, 30
Estero del Bravo, 24
Estero de los Cuarteles, 24
European ships involved in smuggling
  trade, 33

F
Fannin, James W.
  capture and death of, 4, 60, 84–85
  character defense of, 80
  command insecurities, 77
  as Fort Defiance commander, 82
  Goliad, withdrawal to, 76–77
  headquarters changed by, 74
  Houston, S. relations with, 62–63
  Matamoros expedition, role in, 49, 58–
    59, 59, 60, 61, 62, 63, 64, 65, 66
  Matamoros expedition abandoned by,
    67, 68, 73, 82
  men killed under, 85
  Mexía, J. A., correspondence with, 84
  orders, conflicting given to, 74–75, 83
  portrait, 59
  Texas independence question, attitude
    concerning, 68, 83
  Urrea, J. de, information concerning,
    16, 80, 83
  Urrea, J. de underestimated by, 16, 69,
    72, 80
  Victoria, retreat to, 84
Farías, Gregorio Valentín, 30
Farías, Valentín Gómez, 40
federalism, Mexican, Anglo support of,
  79–80
federalists, Mexican
  Anglo Texan relations with, 4, 45, 46,
    47, 48, 52, 67
  centralists versus, 2, 16, 38
  help not forthcoming from, 63, 66,
    68, 77
  Matamoros expedition backed by, 43
  military maneuvers of, 40, 47
  political victories, 15
  Texas establishment as federalist state
    backed by, 7
  Texas rebellion not supported by, 72
  Texas rebellion opposed by, 5, 63–64
  Urrea's side, switch by, 76
Federal Volunteer Army of Texas, 53, 55, 60,
  104–105n3
Fernández, Francisco Vital (General)
  Johnson, F. W. communication with, 73
  intelligence sources concerning, 73,
    74, 76
  Texas rebels fought by, 48
  troops under, 67
  Urrea, J. de aided by, 71
Fernández, José Antonio
  federalist volunteers, call for, 74
  surviving documents issued by, 48

troops raised by, 48, 71
"Volunteers of the Fatherland,"
    reference to, 76
Fernández, Lucas, 31–32
Filisola, Vicente
    army command transferred to, 85
    Garay, F. diary quotes by, 76
    intelligence concerning, 77, 108n21
    Johnson, F. W. attitude toward, 74
    marching conditions described by, 86
    at Matamoros headquarters, 33
    Urrea, J. de, dispute with, 87
Fisher, George "Jorge," 36–37, 46, 68
Florida, U.S. annexation of, 42
foreigners
    imprisonment and execution of, 53
    rights and legal status of, 31, 100n13
Fort Defiance, 4, 82
Fortifications of Matamoros, construction
    of, 13
Fort Lipantitlán, 43, 44–45, 67, 78, 81
Fort Paredes, 23, 33
Fort Texas (later Fort Brown), 89
Fowler, Will, 38, 39, 85, 87, 109n39
free trade zone (Zona Libre), 91
French intervention in Mexico (1862–
    1867), 91
Furber, George C., 19–20

G
Gaines, Edmund Pendleton, 85
Garay, Francisco, 76, 77, 108n21
gardens of Matamoros, 24, 25
gateway to Mexico, Matamoros as, 7, 18,
    27, 90
golden age, 90–93
Goliad
    campaign against, 4, 72, 77, 84
    defense of, 74, 75
    Hispanic citizens of, 56
    under martial law, 46
    Matamoros compared to, 5, 17
    remembering, 6
    residents of, 1–2
    strategic importance of, 43–44, 82
    Viesca, J. M. arrival at, 45
    withdrawal to, 76–77
Goliad Declaration of Independence, 53,
    55, 56, 66
Goliad Massacre

anniversary, tenth of, 89
    factors in, 80–81
    overview of, 4
    survivors of, 22
    Urrea, J. de association with, 69, 84–85
González, Gerardo Palomo, 70
González, Gertrudis Elías, 69
González, José María
    Austin, S. dealings with, 47
    cavalry force joining Urrea, 72
    in Matamoros expedition, 66, 67
    movements of, 54
    Texas cause aided by, 71
    Viesca, J. M. and others aided by, 45, 49
González, Jovita, 87
goods, transport of, 20, 21, 33
Grant, James
    arrest and escape of, 45, 49
    Benavides, P. joining, 73
    character defense of, 80
    defeat and killing of, 78–80, 83
    Dimmitt, P. relations with, 54–55, 56
    historic significance of, 6
    Matamoros expedition, role in, 3–4, 16,
        17, 43, 49, 50, 52, 57
    as Matamoros expedition commander,
        58, 59, 60, 62, 63, 64–65, 66, 67,
        75–76, 77–78
    men killed under, 85
    political views of, 50–51, 79–80
    property and business ventures of,
        50–51
    as self-appointed army commander, 53,
        54, 56
    Urrea, J. de intelligence concerning, 78
    Urrea, J. de underestimated by, 69, 74,
        80
Grant, Ulysses S., 22
Great Comanche Raid of 1840, 87–88
Guerra, José M., 79
Guerrero, Tamaulipas, 89
Gutiérrez de Lara, José Bernardo, 40

H
Hardin, Stephen, 62, 64, 79
heroes, cities named after, 10–11
"Heróica Matamoros" (Heroic Matamoros)
    (city title), 90, 93
Herrera Pérez, Octavio, 7
Herring, Patricia Roche, 70

Hidalgo y Costilla, Miguel, 40
History of Texas (Brown), 3–4
History of Texas and the Texans (Johnson), 50,
   80, 103n11
Houston, Sam
   as army commander in chief, 84
   Dimmitt, P. allegiance to, 52
   jockeying for power by, 75
   Matamoros expedition, attitude
      concerning, 3, 4, 5, 6, 43, 46, 48–49,
      50, 52, 60, 80, 84, 85
   Matamoros expedition command role
      of, 61–64, 65, 66
   Millard, H., dealings with, 54, 104n22
   orders given to, 83
   rumors spread by, 54
   San Jacinto, victory at, 85, 87
   San Jacinto bloodbath, inability to
      control, 80
   speeches by, 62, 63, 64
   supplies, shortage cited by, 53–54
Huracan (term origin), 38
hurricanes and cyclones, 2, 3, 38
Huson, Hobart, 44

I
illegal immigration, 16, 93
immigrants to Texas
   composition of, 15–17, 33, 35
   land acquisition as goal of, 15
   smuggling involvement of, 32, 33
independence movements, Mexican, 6
Indians
   alliances, Mexico seeking, 87
   attacks by, 15, 27, 87–88
   rights and legal status of, 31, 100n13
industrialization, 91–92
intelligence gathering, polyglot population
   and, 35
Irish immigrants to Texas, 16–17, 55
Irish-Mexican intermarriage, 17
Iturbide, Agustín de, 30, 31, 39

J
Jackson, Andrew, 64, 85
Jackson, Jack, 5
Jefferson, Thomas, 42
Johannsen, Robert, 90
Johnson, Francis W. "Frank"
   Austin, S. warnings issued to, 52

defeat of, 78, 83
Fannin, J. W., communication with,
   73–74
flag in possession of, 55
Houston, S. relations with, 62
Matamoros expedition, role in, 3–4, 43,
   49, 51, 52, 54, 57
as Matamoros expedition commander,
   58, 60, 62, 63, 64–65, 66, 73, 77
men killed under, 85
Texas independence question, attitude
   concerning, 68
Urrea, J. de underestimated by, 69, 72,
   74
works of, 50, 80, 103n11

K
Karankawa Indians, 78
Kearney, Milo, 11–12
Kelley, Pat, 31
Kenedy, Mifflin, 90
Kennedy, William, 15
Kentucky Mustangs, 49
Kerr, James, 45
King, Amon B., 76, 84
King, Richard, 90
Kuykendall, J. Hampton, 77

L
La Bahía (Goliad). *See* Goliad
La Bahía presidio (*later* Fort Defiance), 4, 82
Lack, Paul D., 76
Lafon, Antonio, 1, 2, 3, 26
lancers, Mexican, 70, 72, 78–79, 79
land acquisition, push for, 15
land grants, restrictions on, 15, 97n29
land speculation, 43, 51, 54, 60, 66
landings and ports. *See* ports
Laredo, 12
Laso, Carlos, 43, 53, 55
Lawrence, Benjamin, 49
Lemus, Pedro, 33, 73, 74
Lindley, Thomas Ricks, 52–53
Linn, John J., 45, 51, 56
Lipan Apache Indians, attacks by, 88
Long, James W., 40
López de Herrera, Vicente, 30
Los Indios Free Trade Bridge, 92–93
Louisiana, U.S. annexation of, 42

M

Magee, Augustus W., 40

Manchaca, Antonio, 72

Manifest Destiny, 3, 6, 88

matamorenses
American capital and consumer culture impact on, 93
American capitalism embraced by, 37
Carbajal, J. M. J. distrusted by, 90
changing identities and conflicting actions of, 5, 7, 36, 41
Mexican military, relations with, 40–41
military defense challenges faced by, 13
political views of, 36–37
revolts and resistance by, 5, 40, 41
Texas independence impact on, 88–89

Matamoros, Mariano, 7–8, *8,* 31–32

Matamoros area and surroundings, 18–23, *28, 65*

Matamoros blockade, 88

Matamoros city description
after United States-Mexican War, 90–91
post-revolutionary period (1848), *65*
pre-revolutionary period, 23–25

Matamoros, economic importance of, 1, 9–10, 14–15, 27, 30–32, 35–36, 43, 47, 91–93, 100n14

Matamoros expeditions, 1835–1836
authority sought for, 51, 52, 54, 68
carrying out, 54
command of, 56–57, 58–61, 65
concerns regarding, 46, 52
cost of, 84
failure of, 77, 80, 85
historic analysis of, 6
horse need as factor in, 22
little known about, 3–4
maps, *81*
Mexican participation in/support for, 16, 38, 43, 44, 49
oversimplification of, 5
plans made for, 48–50
supplies for, 53–54
sustaining, 75

Matamoros-La Bahía Road, 1–2

Matamoros name
adoption of permanent, 13, 14, 31–32
earliest, 8–9
misspellings, 2, 89–90
and titles, 3, 7, 90

Matamoros occupation, 47, 63, 68, 76, 78, 81, 89

Matamoros origin, 7–9

May, Robert, 6

Mayan Indians, 70

McClintock, William A., 19

McGloin, James, 77

McMullen, John, 76, 77

McMullen and McGloin colony (San Patricio), 16–17

medieval culture, 11–12

Medrano, Manuel, 11–12

Mejía, Francisco, 89

Mexía, José Antonio
cooperation sought by Anglos, 47
correspondence, 83–84
Matamoros expedition command advocated for, 38, 43, 48, 52
Santa Anna, A. L. de opposed by, 37, 40, *45*
Tampico assault by, 44, 46, 48, 49, 103n7

Mexican army, 85–86, 88

Mexican civil war, 38

Mexican colonization of Texas, factors discouraging, 16, 27

Mexican immigrants to Texas, 16

Mexican independence, 14–15, 70

Mexican Revolution (1910–1920), 91

Mexicans. *See also* norteños; Tejanos
Anglos, attitudes toward, 42, 52, 71
imprisonment and execution of, 53

Mexican states, northern, 6

Mexican War of Independence
economic impact of, 10, 27, 31
heroes in, 7–8
key participants in, 70
Matamoros (Refugio) during, 30, 40

mexicano-Tejano dual identity, 6

Mexico
cotton industry in, 92
history, Matamoros role in, 7
independence and establishment of republic, 31
Matamoros campaign of, 5
Matamoros economic importance to, 1, 9–10, 27, 32, 35, 36, 37, 43, 92
Matamoros strategic importance to, 4–5, 33
national government versus Matamoros,

40–41
northern, U.S. occupation of, 90
slavery abolished by, 33, 35, 42, 100–101n20
Spain attempt to reinvade, 13
territorial sovereignty, attempts to defend, 7
Texas, attempts to recapture, 48, 64, 87–88
Texas, loss of, 38, 85–86, 87
Texas independence impact on, 87–88
Texas preservation strategies of, 5
Mexico versus Texas, a Descriptive Novel (Taylor), 15
Mier, 12
Mier y Terán, José Manuel de. See Terán, José Manuel de Mier y
Milam, Ben, 45, 49
Millard, Henry, 54
Miller, Edward L., 40
Miracle, Julián Pedro, 47–48, 64
Molano, Juan Nepomuceno, 13
Montejano, David, 14
Mora-Torres, Juan, 36
Morris, Robert C., 40, 70, 74, 78
muleteers, Mexican, goods transport by, 20, 33
Muslim invaders, Spanish fight against, 10–11
mustangs, sightings of, 22

N
Neill, James, 53, 61, 62, 63, 65
New Orleans Greys, 40, 42, 49, 50. See also San Antonio Greys
norteños
    American capitalism embraced by, 37
    Anglos, attitudes toward, 16
    economic independence of, 28–29
    term defined, 1, 94n2
    Urrea, J. de support won among, 70–71, 76
North American Free Trade Agreement, 93
northern Mexico republic, plot to establish, 58
Nuevo León, city names in, 10
Nuevo Santander, 27–28, 31

O
Order of Guadalupe, 39

Ortiz de Ayala, Simón Tadeo, 35
oxcarts, goods transport with, 21, 33

P
Palacio, Juan Armando de, 12
Palo Alto, battle of, 1846, 3
Paredes y Arrillaga, Mariano, 13
Pearson, Thomas K., 63
Plan of Cuernavaca, 38, 101n4
Plan of Iguala, 30
Plaza de Armas, 9, 24, 25
Plaza Hidalgo, 9
Portilla, José Nicolás de la, 85, 109n39
ports
    along Río Bravo, 18
    establishment, push for, 30
    Matamoros, 14–15, 32, 33, 36
    north of Matamoros, 23
Power, James, 45
Power and Hewetson colony (Refugio), 16
pre-revolutionary period, 1–2, 7–17
Presidio La Bahía, fortification of, 56
Pretalia, Rafael, 78
prohibition, 92
Puerto del Refugio, 30
Punta de Isabel port
    goods unloaded at, 33
    importance of, 18, 19, 29
    smuggling at, 29

R
Racer's Storm (hurricane), 38, 101n3
Raleigh, Eve, 87
Ramírez y Sesma, Joaquin, 53, 77, 85, 108n21
rancheros
    attire of, 20
    as citizen militia, 12, 12–13
    crucial to Urre,a 12, 63, 68, 71, 78, 84
    hearty spirit of, 29–30
ranching, importance of, 36
Refugio (Matamoros's previous name)
    commercial potential of, 30–31
    customs house at, 30–31
    growth of, 29
    during Matamoros expedition, 4, 57, 63
    name and name changes, 9, 31–32
    port at, 30
    residents of, 1–2
    smuggling at, 29

Refugio (Texas)
  battle of, 4, 80–81, *81*, 84
  during Matamoros expedition, 4, 57, 63
Reid, Stuart, 6, 53, 54, 64
Republic of the Rio Grande, 89
Republic of the Sierra Madre, 90
Resaca de la Palma, battle of, 1846, 3
Reséndez, Andrés, 6
Reynosa, 12
Río Bravo
  bridging of cultures by, 91–92
  description of, 18
  flood of 1814, 9
  maps, *19*
  ports on, 30
  settlements along, 9, 15
  travel along, 23, 31
Río Bravo del Norte, 35
Rio Grande
  bridge across, *91*
  bridging of cultures by, 91–92
  transportation and commerce role of, 14
Rio Grande Valley, lower, 18–22
Robinson, James W.
  correspondence, 66, 82, 83
  Fannin, J. W. communication with, 76–77
  Johnson, F. dealings with, 52
  mixed messages sent by, 74, 75
  on Texas independence question, 68
  as Texas provisional lieutenant governor, 42, 51
Rodríguez, Nicolás
  as Fort Lipantitlán commander, 44, 67, 71, 78
  Urrea, J. de's lancers, comments concerning, 79
Ruiz, Ramón Eduardo, 93
Runaway Scrape, 1836, 85

S

Saltillo, 28
San Antonio
  campaign against, 72
  Matamoros compared to, 5
  Santa Anna, A. L. de at, 82, 85
San Antonio Greys, 49, 56, 82. *See also* New
  Orleans Greys
San Jacinto

battle aftermath, 88
  celebrating, 6
  Matamoros compared to, 5, 17
  Mexican defeat at, 3, 85, 87
San Juan de los Esteros Hermosos (name), 9
San Patricio
  battle of, 4, 78, 80–81, *81*
  residents of, 1–2
Santa Anna, Antonio López de
  campaign against, 43, *45, 66*
  capture of, 85, 87
  centralist policies of, 5
  death to foreign rebels ordered by, 84–85
  Fannin, J. W. compared to, 63
  Fannin, J. W. executed by order of, 4
  intelligence concerning, 77, 108n21
  Matamoros attack, projected response to, 73
  Matamoros defense against, attempted, 3
  Matamoros expedition and, 60, 61, 68
  as Mexican president, 38–39
  opposition to, 42, 46, 47, 50, 74
  personal property and memorabilia, 54, 104n22
  portrait, *59*
  revolts against, 37, 39–40, 44
  rise to power, 70
  at San Antonio, 82, 85
  San Antonio possession planned by, 72–73
  Tejano attitudes toward, 83
  Texans' attitude concerning, 4
  Texas invaded by, 72, 74, 77
  Texas preoccupation of, 41
  troop movements, 45
  Urrea, J. de relations with, 69, 70
Santiago Matamoros (St. James the Moor
  Slayer), 10–11, *11,* 12–13
sculpture, monumental at Matamoros, 7
Sea of Mud (Dimmick), 85–86, 87
Sebastián (Enrique González Carbajal), 7
secessionist movements, 89, 90, 100n11
Seguín, Juan, 49
slavery, 33, 35, 42
slaves, runaway, 33, 35, 100–101n20
Smith, David Willard, 27
Smith, Henry
  Houston, S. dealings with, 63, 64

Matamoros expedition, attitude
  concerning, 46, 51, 58, 65, 75
  resignation refused by, 61
  as Texas provisional governor, 42
smuggling trade
  after Matamoros status elevation, 32–33
  attempts to counter, 36
  in Brownsville, 91
  Carbajal, J. M. J. connections with, 90
  drugs, 93
  havens for, 29
  in Refugio, 30
  revenue collected from, 14
  rise of, 29
  in Texas independence aftermath, 88
Spain, 13
Spanish Reconquista, 10–11
squares of Matamoros, 24–25
Staples, Stephen (Esteban) M., 31
steamships, 31
Stillman, Charles, 90
streets of Matamoros, 24, 28
Sutton, Warner P., 91

T
Tamaulipas
  city names in, 10
  name origin, 31, 99n12
  political views in, 72
  U.S. invasion of, 89
Tampico, expedition against, 40, 44, 46, 48,
  49, 103n7
Tarleton, James, 49
Taylor, Creed, 15, 27, 71–72, 73
Taylor, Zachary, 89–90
Tejanos
  Anglos, attitudes toward, 16, 83
  Matamoros expedition supported by, 43
  Texas independence impact on, 88
  as Texas independence supporters,
    55–56
  Texas Revolution, attitudes concerning,
    72
  Texas Revolution deaths of, 79
  Urrea, J. de attempt to gain support
    of, 71
Terán, José Manuel de Mier y, 13, 21, 33, 34
Texans, unrealistic attitude of, 4
Texas
  attempts to keep war out of, 47

industries and commerce, 35–36
maps, 2, 18
march into, 53
Mexican attempt to recapture, 48, 64,
  87–88
Mexican loss of, 38, 85–86, 87
as Mexican state, 7, 15, 27, 35
secessionist movements in, 89, 90,
  100n11
slavery in, 33, 35
U.S. annexation of, 5, 44, 69, 88
Texas (Kennedy), 15
Texas colonists
  in army, 85
  independence movement, attitudes
    concerning, 83
"Texas fever," outbreak of, 15
Texas forces
  defeat of, 80
  goals and philosophy of, 68–69
Texas General Council
  advisory committee of, 74, 75
  condemnation of, 55, 56, 65, 66
  Constitution of 1824 backed by, 58
  dissensions in, 61
  establishment of, 42
  Fisher, G. dealings with, 46
  Goliad Declaration of Independence
    and, 55, 56
  Johnson, F. W. welcomed by, 51
  Matamoros expedition sanctioned by,
    60, 64, 66, 68, 84
  Miracle, J. P. dealings with, 47
  mixed messages sent by, 74, 75, 83
  Robinson, J. W. defense of political
    position, 83
  warning issued to, 52
Texas independence
  aftermath of, 87–89
  colonists divided on, 83
  disadvantages of asserting, 4, 66
  factors contributing to, 6
  federalist sympathizers, professed
    actually behind, 40
  Goliad Declaration of Independence,
    53, 55, 56, 66
  leadership of, 53
  Mexican opposition to, 17, 70, 71, 87,
    89
  Mexico, impact on, 87, 89

provisional government, 42
support growing for, 44
Texas Convention declaration of
    independence, 78, 84
treaty for, 85
war, 38
Texas Navy, 88
Texas provisional government
    division in, 58, 65
    establishment of, 42–43
    Goliad Declaration of Independence as
        indictment of, 56
    Matamoros expedition backed by, 48,
        52
    Matamoros expedition force
        independent of, 54
    paralysis to, 51, 80
Texas rebels
    campaign against, 48, 63, 71
    defeat of, 68
    Matamoros as target for, 42
    Mexican rebel alliance unlikely with,
        48
Texas Republic, 3, 87
Texas Revolution
    in broader revolution context, 6
    deaths, 79
    economic impact of, 32, 100n14
    historical novels concerning, 87, 109n1
    horses and, 22
    impact of, 7
    Matamoros role in, 3–4, 5, 7, 17, 62, 93
    Mexican attitudes concerning, 72
    Mexican political divisions during, 41
    myths concerning, 6
    origin of, 38
    traditional interpretation of, 5–6
    Urrea, J. de role in, 69
Tornel, José María, 69
tourism, 91–92, 93
trade
    American, Mexican dependence on, 88
    benefits of opening, 36
    bridging of cultures through, 91–92
Travis, William B.
    at Alamo, 4, 61, 62, 82
    Fannin, J. W. situation compared to that
        of, 84
    men killed under, 85
    Santa Anna, A. L. de, given warning

concerning, 72–73
Twelve Months Volunteer, The (Furber),
    19–20

U

Union Navy, 91
United States consulate in Matamoros, 14
United States encroachment
    expansionist policy, 42
    Manifest Destiny, 3, 6, 88
    restraining, 27
United States-Mexican War
    factors leading up to, 88
    historical novels concerning, 87, 109n1
    participants, 19, 98n1
    Urrea, J. de involvement in, 70
Urrea, José Cosme de
    Agua Dulce battle victory of, 78–79, 79
    army retreat, response to, 86
    background, 69–70
    Fannin, J. W. defeated by, 60
    Filisola, V., dispute with, 87
    Goliad, victory at (Encinal del Perdido),
        84
    Goliad prisoner execution, attitude
        concerning, 85, 109n39
    Grant, J., attitude concerning, 79–80
    intelligence available to, 71–72, 78, 82
    intelligence concerning, 77, 108n21
    Irish immigrants captured by, 17
    lancers serving under, 70, 72, 78–79, 79
    Matamoros expedition defeated by, 4,
        16, 63, 70–71
    Matamoros occupied by, 68, 76
    Matamoros withdrawal ordered for, 85
    movements of, 77, 83
    nature and elements battled by, 73
    rancheros serving under, 12, 12, 63, 68,
        71, 78, 84
    Refugio, victory at, 84
    reputation of, 69–70
    San Patricio, victory at, 78
    skill of, 80–81
    success, factors in, 81
    Texas recapture for Mexico attempted
        by, 48
    underestimation of, 74
    unifying strategy of, 75, 76
    Victoria occupied by, 85
Urrea, Mariano de, 69

V

Valerio-Jiménez, Omar S., 41, 88–89
Vázquez, Josefina Zoraida, 40, 45–46, 89
vegetation, 18–20, 23
Velasco, treaties of, 87
Veterans International Bridge (Puente
    Internacional Ignacio Zaragoza), 93
Victoria
    colony at, 16
    occupation of, 85
    residents of, 1–2
    retreat, attempted to, 84
    Texas independence aftermath and
        Indian attacks, 87–88
Viesca, José María, 45, 49, 52, 55
Villa de Bustamante (city names), 10,
    96n18
Villa de Hidalgo (city names), 10, 96n18
Villa de Jiménez (city names), 10, 96n18
Villa de Morelos (city names), 10, 96n18
Villas del Norte (Nuevo Santander)
    Indian attacks on, 88
    Mexican advance through, 70
    political views in, 70

population and ranches, 27–28

W

Wagner, Leslie Alice Jones, 110n7
Ward, William, 60, 64, 66, 84
Washington-on-the-Brazos, convention at,
    56, 64
Weber, David J., 6, 28, 37
Westover, Ira, 45, 55
Wharton, John A., 60
wildlife, 22
Williams, Samuel May, 51
winds, description and intensity of, 1,
    25–26
Wislizenus, Frederick Adolph, 20
Wyatt, Peyton S., 56, 62

Y

Yoakum, Henderson K., 50

Z

Zacatecas, 45
Zárate-Ruiz, Arturo, 7, 16, 87, 89, 90
Zavala, Lorenzo de, 44, 47